Fixing Our Government

By

Herbert Pairitz

Preface

This book is dedicated to my brother, Navy Pilot Ensign Harry Pairitz who, like many other members of the working class, gave his life in WWII to preserve our freedom and our wealth.

 In WWII many of the young men gave their lives to prevent Adolph Hitler and Hirohito from taking over our country , which permitted the wealthy big business investors to retain their freedom , businesses and wealth. After the war the big business investors continued to increase their wealth by exploiting the very same working class that saved them from catastrophe in WWII. This was morally and economically wrong. The wealth of this country that the working class worked for, and also died

for in WWII, should be redistributed to the working class and also used to decrease our financial deficit. The greed of big business for money has denied the working class benefits to which they are entitled to under a democratic form of government.

This book is about what a WWII veteran that served in both Europe and the Pacific theaters thinks is wrong with the operation of our government and what should be done about it to correct our predicament. In order to evaluate information you receive you should always consider the source. I am not a politician who makes money by influencing citizens in order to increase my income. I am what you might call the average citizen who is attempting to increase the standard of living of myself and all of the other working- class citizens. I would like you to consider me as a friend who is suggesting an approach to correcting the operation of our government. I want to declare that everything that I have stated below is the truth as far as I can tell and that if the actions that I have suggested were to be taken, the standard of living of the working class and the poor would be greatly increased and they would enjoy prosperity as depicted in any of their recently shattered American dreams. Most citizens only study small segments of the malfunctioning of our government, but I have outlined the overall operation so that they can correctly determine what changes are best for them.

Table of Contents

Page No.

Section 1. What's Wrong With

Our Government

In the last ten years we have experienced a cultural degradation whereby businesses are no longer required to help the American workers and have resorted to reducing their benefits and sending their jobs overseas to the lowest bidder. With all of our resources we would be able to provide prosperity to every citizen, but greedy big business investors chose not to let this happen. The United States Government is not serving all of the people as it should. It is doing exceptionally well for the wealthy business investors, but doing poorly for the working class citizens. And why is this so? The wealthy have the money to invest in their financial futures and assure themselves of financial stability and they influence our government to their advantage. Most working class citizens have to depend upon business owners providing them with a job whereby they can earn a living wage to obtain the necessities of life and possibly a prosperous future. This struggle between the "haves" and the "have-nots" goes way back to the age of the cave man. Back in those days they didn't have a government but probably there were family members that said that if someone is starving you should help them. Today we do have a government and I believe it is the responsibility of our government to give assistance to those that are in a weak financial condition. This could be due to health problems, living circumstances or just a desire to avoid working for a living. I believe our government should assist them all, providing the loafer with only the bare necessities of life. The creators of The Constitution of the United States thought so when they wrote the preamble to" promote the general welfare," which I believe is the underlying meaning of the whole document. Unfortunately there are many people in high government offices that don't believe in this idea and fight it, with very little opposition from politicians, government office holders and the news media. They found out that you don't make much money by promoting the general welfare, you make it by promoting the corporate welfare. Big corporations do not have humane thoughts, just boards of directors who only value their final profit line. A good government should strive to insure that the working- class citizens get a fair share of business profits and that the big corporations are not permitted to exploit them and drive them into poverty. If you want to make a lot of money you are less likely to get it from the wealthy citizens or businesses. But if you can extract just one dollar from each member of the working class by some gimmick or scam you end up with about three hundred million dollars. The easy way to make lots of money is to exploit the working class. The financial spread between the working class and the wealthy in this country has increased greatly since the regulation of businesses has been decreased. According to the Bureau of Labor Statistics the lower 60% of households (which is the working class) possess only 4% of the nation's wealth. This is morally and economically wrong. This unbalance of wealth proves that the wealthy people in this country are taking advantage of the working class people. The wealthy people have money that they will never spend or need, yet some people do not have access to the bare necessities of life. The members of the working class in America are not primarily the victims of circumstances, coincidence or natural economic activities, but are primarily the victims of a planned attack by the wealthy big business investors and politicians who intentionally exploit them to satisfy their greed for money.

So why is our government promoting corporate welfare and ignoring the promotion of the general welfare? Everybody knows the answer, but few people want to talk about it because if you do you lose your contributions from big corporations to government office holders, politicians, the news media and just about everyone else. Even The United States Supreme Court ignored the general welfare in favor of corporate welfare when they concluded that campaign contributions (a form of bribery) were a form of free speech and should not be limited. This further strengthened the control of big corporations over our government. That brings us to the basic number one reason why Congress or the White House cannot get any legislation passed to resolve our economic problems and many other problems. Big corporation money has completely corrupted our government and controls the operation of the government. Currently most of the members of Congress receive large campaign contributions from big corporations. This money is intended to be spent for the benefit of the individual members of Congress, so it is their money to be used to keep them in office, maybe for life. Most of it probably pays for campaign expenses, but it can also be used for making your wife a member of the campaign at $100,000 a year, parties at a night club, personal court costs, etc. The rules are very flexible and they certainly are not enforced. Politicians and officeholders claim they are given this money because the donator likes their ideology and wants to support it. However, if the politician or officeholder reverses his or her ideology the money will be cut off and they both know that, so it is a pure bribe. Another device employed by big business investors to influence office holders is the threat of launching a negative publicity campaign against any office holder that opposes their desires. We no longer have a democratic form of government that is "ruled by the ruled," but have a plutocracy, which is "ruled by money." Our government is corrupt, and so are most politicians and both political parties and many office holders that take bribes and favors from big corporations for complying with their wishes. If you were a member of Congress would you pass a bill on complete campaign finance reform where the taxpayers finance all campaigns or would you choose to receive a slush fund of about five million dollars a year from big business to keep you in office indefinitely? Most of the members of Congress have chosen the latter, and the working class takes a big hit! Government offices have been purchased by spending overwhelming amounts of money on campaigns and it has been estimated that members of Congress now spend over half of their minimal working hours on fundraising. There is no recovery in sight until we take the money out of politics and the control of our government is given back to the citizens.

One thing that has been hurting the working class severely in recent years is the price gouging. Prices have not gone up on a gradual increase like they used to, but we now get individual increases of 50% or more without any associated event or any explanation. The price of ground beef and milk have doubled within the last year, and the price of potatoes has quadrupled. This year the price paid to the farmers for potatoes has been cut in half, but the big business distributors can charge whatever they want because Congress is controlled by big business. Our politicians call this normal supply and demand; "the working class supplies the money and big business demands a large profit". There is not much discussion about the severe price increases, except for gas prices, a product that everyone is forced to purchase no matter what the price is. Our exports of gasoline, diesel and jet fuel are a huge 88 billion dollars a year. As a member of the working class I say that we should not export a drop of gasoline or other fuels to other countries but should sell it in the United States and not let big business investors use it to exploit the working-class citizens. The demand for oil and gasoline is down and the supply is up and yet the selling price is very high due to the future traders and excessive big oil company profits. Finding new fuels and increasing drilling will not solve the problem. The big business investors and future traders will just increase prices on the new fuels in order to increase their profits. Price gouging has been greatly increased by the reduction in business regulations by the Bush Administration and the failure to correct this problem in the Obama

Administration.   As a result, businesses have concluded that they can keep raising prices and they all make more money, rather than try to compete with each other by lowering prices. In the past years prices went down with a depressing economy, but this time it is different, prices are skyrocketing.   A federal budget of 4.1 billion dollars is available to the wealthy pharmaceutical companies and when they develop the new drug the taxpayers of the United States are charged twice as much for it as the citizens of Canada. The Federal Government tells us that inflation is under control, but it appears to be way out of control. The government does not want to raise the interest rates to decrease inflation because businesses want the low rates for lucrative financial investments.   All of this inflation is particularly hard on senior citizens whose retired earnings are worth less than ten percent of what they were worth at the time of retirement

For the past ten years or so we have been exercising a new policy of sending jobs to foreign countries to obtain cheaper labor. When IBM outsourced jobs to India profits went up, the stock market went up and the working class lost another ten thousand jobs. General Electric and Apple both employ most of their people outside of the United States and General Electric plans to invest two billion dollars in China. Investors now have a way of increasing the business economy and decreasing the working class economy all at the same time. Businesses create most of the jobs in this country, but under a democratic government they should have a responsibility to pay employees a fair living wage whenever possible and they should not be allowed to replace American workers with cheaper foreign workers, which is big business's best way to increase profits. This is a direct violation of our Constitution which dictates promoting the general welfare

Our trading with China has a lot of devastating results that are weakening our number one status as a leader of world affairs. Not only does our huge trade deficit with China reduce our financial structure but it also strengthens the financial power of a communistic dictatorship that has an agenda to someday crush the United States into submission. They knocked down one of our commercial airliners and we ended up paying them for caring for the hostages they took. We should stop trading with China and Viet Nam no matter what it costs us and notify China that the cost and humiliation of the airline incident is exactly the same as out trade deficit and then cancel it. What a price this country is paying just so the big corporations can replace American workers with cheaper foreign workers and obtain excessive profits. Yes, the American people got lower prices when we first started trading with China but they don't anymore. In fact, prices have increased drastically. The only people that obtain an advantage trading with China are China and the big corporations that distribute Chinese products in this country. China's workers don't have human rights or receive a living wage, and they still keep the value of their money low so they can make even more money trading with us. When trading with $2/hr. countries like China there is also the threat of bringing contaminated products into the United States. We have had this situation with food, drugs and toys. The country of Panama had received some glycerin from China that was contaminated and used it to make cough medicine for their hospitals. As a result one hundred people died. This is just another reason for not trading with unregulated countries like China.

Failure to stop illegal immigration has resulted in loss of jobs by legal citizens and reductions in pay, such as the meat cutting industry going from $21/hr. wages to $9/hr. Illegal immigrants compete with working- class U.S. citizens for education, health care, jobs and welfare. The state of California spends 10.5 billion dollars each year to support these illegal immigrants, which amounts to about $1,200 from each taxpayer. Big business and some politicians promote illegal immigration for the cheaper labor. President Obama stated that giving the twelve to twenty million illegal immigrants in this country a path to citizenship is the humane thing to do. He ignored considering what was humane about U.S. workers giving up their jobs and higher wages and paying higher taxes to provide for Mexico's poverty population, plus the competition for education, health care, etc. If we give this large group of illegal immigrants amnesty just think what it will do to the influx of poverty-stricken people from Mexico, especially since we do not enforce our borders and never will with such an incentive to become U.S. citizens. The Latinos are now the largest ethnic group in the United States and, unfortunately, they vote as a block. The legal immigration of Latinos should be stopped until such time as the illegal immigrants have been controlled. We need to start with the main cause of illegal immigration which is the jobs they get here, but businesses want them for the cheaper labor costs and big business controls our government. I can put the words "big" and "business" adjacent to each other even though it forms one of those political dirty words outlawed by the big corporations. When politicians want to promote legislation to benefit big business they call it "small business," and then give the benefit to big business too.

We need more border guards and fences, not virtual fences that notify you after the illegal immigrants get over the border. A lot of our money was spent on virtual fences that proved to be a bust. But that is standard procedure in our form of government, the politicians and businesses make the money and the citizens pay the bill. This is like so many things about politics and government that you cannot understand. The only way you can understand what's going on is if you check to see who is making money. In this case, as usual, it is politicians, lobbyists and businesses. They don't care that it harms the working class because they are making money by providing a source of cheaper labor to businesses, and politicians are also seeking the votes of the Latino population. We working class people strive for laws that upgrade our standard of living. Years ago that was enough to accomplish a goal. But now we have the problem of getting the laws enforced. Who ever thought the politicians would pull this trick on us? We obtained our laws preventing illegal immigration but politicians are preventing the laws from being enforced. They also have another trick. The House of Representatives can just not fund a law and it doesn't get enforced. Both of these legislative tricks are unreasonable but the control of our government is not in the control of the people so nothing can currently be done about it.

We are all aware of the fact that our economy is in bad shape. During the Bush Administration our economy was split into two separate units. There is the big business investment economy and the working class economy. The former is doing exceptionally well, but the latter is doing poorly. The reason for this split is that big corporations had received the "go ahead" from the Bush Administration to replace

American workers with cheaper foreign workers. This meant that the working class economy would lose millions of jobs, but that action was accepted by the Bush Administration and the Republican Party and was not changed when the Democrats took over Congress and the White House. This seems pathetic, because now they are saying "where did the jobs go?" Well, they went to foreign countries, but big corporation money doesn't want this fact discussed by politicians and news commentators and it is rarely done, and never in any great detail. The approach taken by our politicians is to not take back those jobs given to foreign countries but to get off that subject and suggest getting the jobs by some other means. The means they have chosen are inoperable. Spending taxpayer money on a stimulus program creates very few new good permanent jobs. Many businessmen have admitted that they cannot create new jobs if they get more money. The only thing that can create new jobs is an increase in demand. If we manufacture and sell products right here in the United States the demand will increase enormously. Increasing jobs in the service industries will not resolve the problem either. We need permanent jobs that pay a living wage like manufacturing jobs. Many working class people have two or three service industry jobs and still can't regain their old standard of living. Certainly giving tax breaks to the wealthy will not create new jobs. They will just invest the money in some financial enterprise because the demand for their products or services is not there. If they create any jobs it probably will be overseas where the manufacturing is going on. Tax breaks to the working class will not create jobs either, but it sure will help them survive. Many wealthy citizens don't care if the working class survives. They want a population comprised of the rich and the poor like Mexico.

Some politicians say we will increase jobs if we spend more money on education, but they are decreasing the amount we spend on education. Unfortunately the graduates may have to seek their jobs in foreign countries, where some of our best jobs have been relocated. Then there is the foreign worker visa program that permits foreigners to live here and take jobs away from the higher paid American workers. A lot of them over-stay their visas, but running them down is not a high priority. Businesses claim that they cannot find workers here with the necessary qualifications. Even if that were true, I believe that businesses should be required to train the new employees needed, as General Electric plans to do in China. One of the highest priorities of our government should be to provide permanent well-paying jobs to its citizens. It kind of fits in with our Constitution preamble of promoting the general welfare. Politicians like to say that the United

States will obtain more jobs by being more productive. We are normally more productive than most foreign countries. That requires major investments in capital equipment. In recent years we reported a large productivity increase of 3.5 percent. That number gets lost when you compare it to an American labor cost of over 1000 percent greater than many foreign labor costs.

That brings up the subject of the United States joining the World Trade Organization. Many foreign countries that we trade with have a manufacturing labor cost of less than $2 /hr., while we have a manufacturing labor cost of over $20 /hr. Politicians like to say that we will get jobs back by competing with those foreign countries. That is impossible and that is why our trade deficit is alarmingly out of control. The entire news media and particularly TV find nothing wrong with globalization of our trading. It is accepted by the news media and politicians because it is needed by big corporation money. Unfortunately global trading has devastated the working class economy in this country because we cannot compete with $2/hr. labor costs. Another cause of our loss of jobs is the unfair trade agreements that have been entered into with other countries. One good example is the North American Trade Agreement which gives all sorts of advantages to the other countries and very few to the United States. Most people will agree that NAFTA has cost the U.S. millions of jobs as hundreds of manufacturing plants have been moved to Mexico and other countries. China has a trade agreement with us whereby we must pay a 25 percent tariff on any cars we might sell in China. If someone should suggest that we use tariffs to protect our markets the Republicans would label it as protectionism, which is one of the dirty words they have established in political discussions. It isn't enough that China also has a less that $2 /hr. labor cost to compete with us plus the unfair devaluing of their dollar, they want to get all they can from our negotiators. Why does this happen? As I said before, people are making money. The negotiators, the politicians and the businesses all received generous compensations. As usual, the working class is paying the price for these generous compensations. We have lost millions of jobs that are very difficult to get back, especially if big corporation money controls our government. Thus we have the split in our economy. The greedy activities of big businesses and the politicians have resulted in a new economic system whereby the best method of increasing profits for the big corporations, outsourcing American jobs, has also become the best way to devastate the working class economy. Reports on the economy are rather meaningless because politicians don't want to report separately on the business economy and the working class economy, which are now opposites.

In recent years we almost completely lost our automobile manufacturing industry to foreign competition. General Motors, Chrysler and Ford were all on the ropes and the government had to bail them out. They are doing a little better now because they are using more cheaper foreign made parts like Toyota. This sends more jobs to foreign countries, but they will never be the revenue producing industry that they had been in past years. The city of Detroit Michigan is in terrible financial ruin. Foreign manufacturers with lower labor costs have been allowed to assemble their cars in the U.S. but the parts, where most of the money resides, are manufactured in those foreign countries. A primary example of this was Toyota, but they also experienced losses of sales to countries like China. South Korea has finally broken into our car sales market with their new Hyundai which is bad news to the American car manufacturing industry. If we don't stop the sale of foreign produced cars and parts in the U.S. we will eventually lose the entire American car industry, like we recently almost did.

In summary of Section 1, our government is not promoting the general welfare but, instead, is promoting the corporate welfare. The unequal distribution of the wealth has devastated the working class. Politicians are allowing big business to exploit the working class citizens by replacing American workers with foreign workers, etc. in payment for campaign contributions and other favors, and in defense against any negative publicity campaign by big business investors. The huge amounts of money spent in political campaigns and political activity has completely corrupted our government. In addition, we have price gouging, severe inflation, trading with $2/hr. countries, the illegal immigration burden for the working class, unfair taxing of citizens and deceiving the citizens in order to exploit them.

Section 2. Financial Occupations

Detrimental to Our Economy

If you want to make a lot of money without exerting much effort what kind of a job should you look for? One approach is to be a middleman where you put yourself between someone who has something of value to offer to the public and someone who is willing to purchase that item of value. You don't want to provide products or services because that requires a lot of effort, time and money. You want to just handle a money transfer and make a profit. Money manipulation is the process of creating more money without giving anything of value like products or useful productive services. Today there are millions of jobs in this category in the United States, and perhaps even half of the population. The jobs are not just available to individuals but have become major industries. One good example is the futures trading market. Individuals or companies bid on the future price of certain commodities but never take delivery of the product or service. Individuals or companies bid on the future price of barrels of oil in this unproductive occupation. They offer no benefit to the public and merely raise prices. Some individuals have made up to three billion dollars in a year by futures trading. This results in high prices and excessive inflation, which creates a financial loss to the working class. Both houses of Congress held separate committee hearings on gasoline and oil prices and came to the same conclusion that rising prices were primarily due to futures trading and not supply and demand. Big business money stopped any correction of this problem. Gasoline prices are also manipulated by refineries. If they have a problem at the refinery they don't lose money as they naturally would. Instead, they raise their prices and eventually make even more money. When one refinery raises prices they all do, and don't think this isn't pre-arranged. Unrest in the middle-east should not raise the price of gasoline in the U.S. until some catastrophe actually occurs and the demand actually increases or the supply drops, but the traders are looking for an excuse to raise prices so we get an increase in price immediately. Of course, when the catastrophe doesn't happen the price does not go back down. The same thing occurs with the refineries that never lower the prices back down when the refinery is repaired. Actually, the gasoline being sold at the time the refinery went down should not be subject to a price increase, but the refineries can't wait to get the extra money. Our government should take control of a critical resource like oil and gasoline that citizens are forced to purchase and act as a single payer to obtain the lowest prices in a global market. We should not allow profit- oriented corporations to control and manipulate the price of resources that affect all of our lives and permits them to exploit the working class.

Most politicians contribute nothing of value to the public and spend their time working for personal financial gains by helping big business investors to exploit the working-class citizens by outsourcing jobs, avoiding corporate taxes, etc. Most politicians are avoiding the changes that would help the working class to regain prosperity and are resorting to gridlock to ensure that nothing is accomplished by either party. They are not just not helping the working class, but are making sure that no one else can help them. All of the money wasted by politicians is obtained indirectly from the taxpayers.

The Federal Reserve System gives business extremely low interest rates, which they use to invest in large financial programs that do nothing for the working class economy. With one-half percent interest rates the citizens, and especially the retired senior citizens, lose a critical source of income, the working class are encouraged to go further into debt to take advantage of the low rates and inflation increases. These extremely low interest rates actually hurt the working class in order to provide give-away interest rates to the big business investors. Financial businesses should be confined to commercial transactions and not speculation and gambling with someone else's money. The Federal Reserve System is looking out for the wealthy investors and certainly not the working class, and by no coincidence it is usually managed by someone from Wall Street.

Huge amounts of government funds are spent each year to give subsidies to businesses supposedly to insure their success. This is a questionable practice which has been going on for years and has become more of a political payoff device. Many of these subsidies have been initiated through "earmarks", which are merely inserted into any unrelated bills as a favor to the local voters or friendly big corporations. This is a scam which should be discontinued. Our states and cities are slashing budgets by reducing salaries and laying off policemen, firemen, teachers and other needed services, and at the same time the Federal Government is giving subsidies to the five largest profit making companies which happen to be oil companies. They are not about to fail, but these companies and their affiliated politicians and lobbyists can sure use the money. The government should only loan money to critical industries that are about to go into bankruptcy but should not merely give money to any business. Big corporations don't have to pay federal income taxes if they move their corporate locations to a foreign island or country. This well publicized tax loophole is desired by the big corporations, and the politicians chose to force the working class to make up for the losses in tax revenues.

The common practice of making money in the United States and then investing it in some other country is not in the best interest of the working class. Money that is earned through the labor of our citizens should be reinvested in the United States to strengthen our economy, not the economy of some other country that offers lower labor rates or lower taxes to big business investors. Countries like China, Mexico, Canada, Vietnam and Ireland welcome this economic boost, but the United States would also welcome it and dearly needs it to help our devastated working class and poor citizens. Some of these countries that are being assisted economically are communistic dictatorships that deny their workers living wages and human rights. These practices of replacing our workers and avoiding our taxes should be stopped. Under our current system any President or Congressman that tries to stop it will be left out in the cold financially by big business.

Congress has also failed to properly regulate financial businesses. Interest rates of over 30% are not unusual. We should return to the good old days when over 7% was illegal. People were recently sold mortgages for which they did not financially qualify and were unable to make the payments and eventually lost their homes. Adjustable mortgages should not have been permitted. Mortgages should not be bundled and sold overseas. There is the whole area of money manipulation where big corporations and individuals reap huge profits without providing any real benefit or service to the working class. Banks have increased their leverage of capital on loans from ten times to thirty times, which increases inflation. They are actually creating money, like the government printing presses. There should be zero leverage because no one should be permitted to loan out money they do not possess. Commercial banks should not be permitted to engage in speculation.

Wall Street takes unethical advantage of their customers by gambling against their own offerings, investing in questionable offerings like derivatives and swaps and making our investment structure dependent on other countries. All of them are protected by the government with FDIC, and bailouts when they get caught overextending themselves. Wall Street does more harm than good to the working class in this country, plus the threat of a pending market crash that will devastate our economy. They may supply capital to start new businesses, but banks should be doing all of that and not greedy money manipulators who create profits by devious methods. In the long run it is not right to bail out these unethical financial institutions. They are back doing the same things with no new regulations and getting even bigger and richer so we become even more dependent upon them, waiting for the next market crash. The Dodd-Frank Wall Street Reform and Consumer Protection Act was passed by Congress to increase regulations and create the Consumer Financial Protection Bureau to protect consumers on mortgages, credit cards and payday loan shops. Now the Republican House of Representatives is preventing the funding for the new bill. Wall Street purchased and resold unsupported loans that could not be repaid back in 2008 and the housing market crashed. The Wall Street traders made millions in profits at the expense of the homeowners and taxpayers. It gave them the opportunity to get the prices low so that they could start the price-raising cycle all over again. What the working class really needs is a bill to shut down Wall Street and let the banks handle all of the investment loans for businesses. Wall Street should not be creating money at the expense of the working class. Wall Street represents a complete industry of middlemen money manipulators that should not be allowed to exist in a democracy or any form of fair government.

Then there are the lobbyists, over forty thousand of which reside in Washington D.C. alone, many of them having been government office-holders at one time. They lobby representing businesses and negotiate a price that will be paid to office holders to favor the desires of the big corporations. The activities of the lobbyists are detrimental to the working class since they help big corporations take control of our government so they can exploit the working class. They are another group of influential people that are promoting the corporate welfare rather than the general welfare. Indirectly the taxpayers are paying their salaries since the big corporations are obtaining tax breaks and other favors valued far greater than money paid to the lobbyists. Lobbyists get the opportunity to talk directly to government office holders to influence them, but the average citizen does not get that much representation because he or she has no money to give them for the meeting. This is unequal protection,but the United States Supreme Court only enforces it when they want to promote a political party, like the election of the President in 2000.

Insurance companies perform a service when they stick to the original basis for this occupation. The primary justification for insurance was to provide a large pool of people who can't afford to pay for a financial disaster that strikes an individual or business such as losing one's home due to a fire. In order to make more money insurance companies have injected themselves as middlemen and merely pay the bills for people, taking out administrative costs and an excessive profit. A good example of this type of operation is the HMOs selling insurance policies that ended up doubling our health care costs as compared to the government controlled health care systems of all of the other industrialized countries. Their latest insurance scam is to insure people against paying automobile repair costs. They advertise that you won't have to pay the high costs of failure of a transmission and other high priced repairs, which rarely occur. But you will have to pay their monthly fees plus their administrative costs and a profit every month for sure. People should only insure potential losses that are catastrophic and that they cannot afford. To insure losses one can afford is a financially losing activity. Car repair insurance is a scam that is just getting started. It is another example of insurance companies selling people insurance that is not financially justified. This is another case of middleman money manipulators. At some time in the future we should consider a government takeover of supplying insurance to citizens to take advantage of savings in advertising, profits and administrative costs associated with a single system rather than thousands of separate systems.

To conclude our evaluation of questionable financial institutions we certainly should consider the stock market. Is the stock market operation good for the working class? I would say certainly not. The stock market offers people an opportunity to earn higher profits than regular lending institutions, but then there is a greater risk of losing a little, or losing a lot. The average citizen is at a disadvantage in trading stocks as compared to the wealthy investors who obtain inside information on which stocks are about to go up or down, which businesses are about to increase or decrease in value, what changes in current events are about to effect the market, etc. The activities of the stock market creating money by merely increasing the prices of stock is another source of inflation through money manipulation. Some of the working class –citizens are making money this easy way, which is the wrong way for our society. Some of the larger stock market trading companies actually cause huge losses to other traders with their computer controlled trading programs and huge amounts of money that can force a market crash and make a bundle. And then there is the big one where inside traders are informed when the market is about to crash instead of after it crashes, and this is certainly unfair to the working class traders. Of course, the basis for the stocks are to provide money to expand businesses, but that can be provided by banks without engaging in speculation and creating inflation and giving advantages to insiders. The working class have become another source of revenue for the money-makers. This is another case of the redistribution of the wealth in the wrong direction and manufacturing money instead of earning it.

All of the financial occupations that are detrimental to the working class economy discussed above have been used by big business investors to exploit the working class and enrich the wealthy investors. The goals of the wealthy investors is to reduce those good manufacturing jobs and replace them with money manipulation investment jobs that do very little for the working class and cause excessive inflation.

In summary of Section 2, regulation of businesses has been very weak and caused a collapse of our mortgage market, a decrease of value of our homes and many other financial disasters. Money is being manipulated by middlemen like future traders who profit by merely raising prices without contributing anything of value in their transactions. It is conceivable that over half of our population are employed in this " money creation" type of business. The resulting inflation is devastating to the working class citizens. The Federal Reserve System is helping big businesses but not the working class. There are many government policies and business activities that hurt the working class, such as subsidies, grants, tax loopholes, investing in other countries, high interest rates over 7%, speculation by banks and lobbyists activities.

Section 3. Questionable Use of The
United States Armed Forces

Our armed forces were established to protect the United States from being harmed by any other nation or group of people that may become aggressive. This was true in World War II and we fought that war successfully because it was justified and we had no other reasonable choice. Since then we have been attacked by only one small group of terrorists called al-Qaida. We have made some aggressive actions against al-Qaida, but have not been successful in completely eliminating their threat. Politicians and government leaders have used this threat to promote aggressive military activity by the United States just as was done to promote fighting communism in past years. Not having been directly threatened by any country the United States Government took it upon itself to police the world and invaded Korea and Vietnam with the intention of stopping the spread of communism. Later we invaded Iraq because someone thought they might have weapons of mass destruction, and Afghanistan because the Taliban and about one hundred members of Al-Qaida were disrupting Afghanistan. The citizens of the United States have paid an awful price for those wars in lives and money. Some people say we were fighting for freedom. The only freedom that was involved was the freedom of opposing factions to kill each other in a civil war. The only groups that gained something from those wars were the businesses that got the supply contracts and the people that ended up with the sixty billion dollars of our money that just disappeared through fraud and cheating. What used to be armed forces functions like kitchen duty (KP) and protection of visitors were handled by government contracts to private parties, which are extremely expensive. One of the local kitchen police (KP) employees blew himself up and some of our soldiers were killed, but the contracts still continue because there is money to be made. The visitor protection contractor, Blackwater, murdered a group of Iraq citizens but was never properly punished and continued their business in Iraq. There were over six thousand separate contractors in Iraq employing more people than our total armed forces. Both Iraq and Afghanistan have been in a permanent civil war for years, so no American citizens should ever visit there or live there. Thus there is no need for a U.S. Embassy in Iraq that costs the taxpayers a billion dollars to construct and six million a year to operate. What a money-making operation for greedy businesses to exploit the taxpayers. We should have separated the three fighting factions in Iraq and gotten out of there, but that would have stopped the money flow of the war contracts.

We did not stop the spread of communism in China or Vietnam. In fact, we have been bolstering the financial status of both countries, Vietnam by letting them supply us with most of our underwear and China by supplying us with about everything else. If I had lost a friend or relative in Korea or Vietnam fighting communism I would feel awfully bad about our trading with either country. The scary part about our trading with China is that with the huge trade deficits in their favor they are becoming financially strong to the point that sometime in the near future they will exceed the United States in financial strength as well as military strength.

The United States has forces spread around the world in Germany, Korea, Japan and other places. There is no reason why we should take on the expense of those wasted forces.

Korea is the only one under a threat, but so are many countries in Africa and elsewhere and we can't afford to cover them all, nor should we take on the financial burden and the risk to our soldiers. Also, the United Nations was established to police the world and we should let them do that and support them. The only thing we know for sure is that some businesses are making money off of those occupying forces. The United States has a huge budget to support our armed forces, the largest in the world by a considerable amount. Rather than taking money from education, police forces and other needed services to cover our financial deficits why can't we cut the defense budget considerably? We should not borrow money from China to police the world as we are now doing. The control of Congress and the White House by big corporation money makes all this possible.

The Congress, the White House, political parties and the politicians have used the threat of terrorists to expand our armed forces around the world by employing scare tactics. We certainly cannot eliminate the terrorists by invading countries like Iraq and Afghanistan and forcing ourselves into some other country's civil war. If we defeat the terrorists in these countries they are very flexible and will move their operations to some other location. Fighting them will only make them more resolved to perform acts of terror against us, as will invading and occupying Islamic territories. We end up killing citizens of foreign countries, which is ruthless. And there is the fact that our troops are put at a dangerously unfair advantage because they cannot identify the enemy until after he shoots at them. So why are all of these politicians continually promoting wars? They do it to get war contracts for their supporters and political power and financial gain for themselves. President Eisenhower warned us about the dangers of the military industrial complex.

In summary of Section 3, our armed forces are not utilized to protect our citizens from invasion by other aggressive countries as originally intended, but are employed by our politicians to provide huge business profits to greedy corporations that are willing to squander the lives of our young men and women and the taxpayer money to achieve their financial goals. In Iraq we spent almost a trillion dollars and lost about 4,500 troops and the civil war is continuing as it would have without our intervention and might have subsided sooner. Saddam

Hussein killed a lot of his people but none of ours, and he prevented a civil war and controlled the terrorists and the citizens. The new government is very corrupt and very unlikely to provide its citizens with a democracy or freedom. Policing the world is highly detrimental to our working-class citizens.

Section 4. What is the True Value

Of Our Political System ?

A good portion of our overall economy is spent on our politicians and the political parties. What value is actually obtained? To start with, the politicians are not serving the citizens of this country. Let's look at their allegiances in priority sequence. First of all, they do what's best for themselves, like making as much money as they can. Second, they do what's best for the big corporations that give them large contributions and other favors. Third, they do what's best for the political party to which they belong and obtain support for re-elections. Fourth, they do what's best for the citizens that vote them into office. It is obvious that money is what controls their daily activity. Take away the money and you may be able to get them to do what's best for the average citizens. Of course, the best thing would be to take away the politicians. Then there is the federal financial debt ceiling whose only real purpose is to provide politicians with more power and money. It does not reduce the spending, but does give the political parties a wedge to force the other party to "cut a deal" that will reduce benefits to the working class. Most politicians are not doing a good job for the working class in this country. All they do well is to assist the big corporations in exploiting the working class by replacing American workers with cheaper foreign workers and other programs that make more money for big corporations and themselves. One of the main desires of politicians is to become a major office holder so they can make even more money through large campaign contributions from big business and also from the voters. Or they could become lobbyists and take on the lucrative job of shielding the big corporations from having to do the incriminating dirty work of negotiating with Congress and the White House for tax breaks, subsidies and other favors.

Over the years, politicians have organized the citizens into separate political parties so they could create an overwhelming force to vie for the financial support of big business investors and to lock in the votes of the citizens. Now that campaign funding has become a primary factor in winning elections their goal is not to represent the average citizen, but to accumulate as much money as they can. The Republican Party advertises the promotion of certain ideas that are detrimental to the working class. One that wealthy people should be given large tax reductions. Two that businesses should not be regulated at all. Three that our budgets should be trimmed by decreasing the benefits given to the working class. In spite of these shocking disclosures they still receive the support of many working class citizens that have been influenced by TV and the news media who get their money from the big corporations, understandably averaging eighty percent of their political contributions to the Republican Party and only twenty percent to the Democratic Party. That makes sense because the Republicans give big business about sixty percent more benefits than the Democrats give. Most members of the working class will promote a principle of their party even if it harms the working class and often, them personally. Both political parties have decided to accept the contributions and favors from big corporations in exchange for permitting them to exploit the working class by moving their jobs to foreign countries, etc. Both political parties have also decided to expend most of their energies to gain control of the Congress and the White House no matter what it costs the citizens. For instance, the Republicans are against any type of government controlled health care plan which would be a huge benefit to the working class. And the Democrats choose to give a path to citizenship, or amnesty, to the twelve to twenty million illegal immigrants in this country in order to obtain the Latino vote. So the two parties' primary objective is not to promote the general welfare but to stop the other from enjoying any success in passing bills. There is another device that the parties can utilize to increase their power and decrease the effectiveness of a democratic form of government and that is the current trend of voting as a solid block. Recently the Republicans have been employing this tactic on a regular basis and it has been very successful. They have gotten President Obama on the defensive where he has been pleading for them to consider compromising on contentious issues. The Democrats are a little more difficult to get to vote in a block. They are in control of the administration and are not as desperate and don't have as much financial support of big corporations but do have the lesser support of the labor unions.

Members of Congress and politicians

often promote compromising to pass a bill. Compromising is a political tool used to give something to the opposition in exchange for them agreeing to vote for the bill. This degrades the bill and should not be done. It is just another one of the prices we pay to have political parties. They talk about compromising when passing legislation, but that only results in trade-offs that fashion a watered- down bill like the health care bill that ended up being unacceptable to the liberal Democrats and a boon to the HMOs, who some claim actually wrote the bill. One of the Democrats said he wouldn't vote for the original bill with the public option because he knew it wouldn't get the sixty votes needed in the Senate. That's a weak excuse for justifying the contributions he received from the big corporations. Members of Congress should not pass legislation by compromising or "cutting a deal" but should only consider what is beneficial for the average citizen. Another way that political parties degrade our democracy is to accept amendments to a bill that are not related to the content of the bill but are use by the opposing political party to get something for themselves and big business investors as a bribe for their support of the bill. An example is the Republicans demanding large tax cuts for the wealthy or they will defeat the budget bill that is needed to keep the government financially in operation. All amendments to bills should be required to have a direct relation to the bill without the manipulation by political parties.

Our political system has evolved, not based

on promoting the general welfare per our Constitution, but based on cashing in on the vulnerability of the working-class citizens to get their money and their votes. The main incentive of our system of politics has been the profits available to big business and the politicians. Big business contributes money and favors to politicians so they are permitted to exploit the working class. The politicians accept contributions from both big corporations and the citizens and still manage to convince many voters that the politicians are serving their interests. Part of this deceit is made possible by the distracting battle between the parties. The working-class voters of the two political parties should not be fighting each other, but they all should be fighting the big business investors who are exploiting them.

The two major political parties in the U.S. have been established so that small groups of politicians can influence large groups of citizens and make money by soliciting contributions from the citizens as well as big business investors who are willing to pay for the lucrative support of the supposedly citizens' representatives. The first step of this setup is to convince the citizens that this particular political party is looking out for the financial interests and well being of the citizens, even if their true actions are to make more money for the politicians that control the party. This is verified by the fact that politicians aid big corporations in exploiting the working class with such programs as replacing American workers with cheaper foreign workers and reducing corporation taxes. They promote free trade to fight the regulation of businesses and permit them to exploit the working class. One of the most effective devices of the political parties is to divide the interests of the citizens so they end up fighting each other's party rather than fighting big business investors who are exploiting the working class and corrupting our government with their money. More and more we see situations where one party will refuse to agree to a benefit for the working class in order to prevent the other party from passing a successful bill. Political parties are a nonproductive business and they offer nothing of value like products or useful services, and making money takes precedence over representing the citizens. Citizens should not be locked into political parties but should vote and act independently based on what is best for themselves personally and give priority to what is best for the average citizen. When you join a political party you give up the right to represent yourself individually in the governing process.

In order to achieve their monetary goals politicians will resort to lies, but they prefer to just deceive people by clouding the issue. One example of this is when a politician proposes to resolve our economic problem by being more competitive. That sounds great, unless you think further and come to the conclusion that in order to be competitive in global trading we would have to reduce our labor costs to less than $2/hr. Nevertheless, members of that political party all continually repeat that statement. When the news commentators on TV ask politicians a question they rarely answer yes or no. What they usually do is change the subject and quickly fire back with several other of their favorite arguments for which there is not time to question. In a recent interview with a member of Congress, he was asked if he would vote no on the contested funding bill if his amendment to kill funding for Planned Parenthood programs was omitted. In his answer he included a statement that he was more interested in reducing the taxes. What he actually wanted to do was decrease the taxes for only the wealthy taxpayers and make the low income working class pay for their own Planned Parenthood counseling. They do the same thing with the general phrase "reducing spending", when they mean to only reduce spending on worker's benefits. Politicians also use the word "immigration", when they want to confuse the word "immigration" with "illegal immigration". This is very misleading to the public, but most news commentators permit it. Some commentators permit it because they are overwhelmed by the number of unrelated statements and don't want to wander off of the subject. The Republicans in the House of Representatives ended up voting against that contested funding bill in a block and some Democrats voted against it too. How could they all do this to the working class? The answer is our new standard answer for unreasonable political events – money from big corporations.

The Tea Party has recently evolved out of citizens who recognize that our government is not functioning properly and is not giving them the benefits that they need. So their intentions are to protest against the existing administration. Since neither the Republican administrations nor the Democratic administrations are able to give them what they want I believe they will be switching their complaints to whichever administration is in power. Of course, since the Republican Party has started to back them financially with big corporation money many of them will remain affiliated with that party only. When the Tea Party has a demonstration in Washington D.C. I don't think the individual members pay their own expenses, they are probably financed by big corporation money through the Republican

Political Party. These are a group of people who know something is wrong, but they each kind of go their own way as indicated by the signs they display. Of course, some are influenced by Republican politicians who have convinced them that big government, socialism and regulation of businesses are bad for them. The politicians make sure there are no signs saying "take the money out of politics", which happens to be the number one cause of most all of their problems. There are also no signs on the evils of Wall Street, big business exploitation of workers, corruption, etc. They are sticking by the rules set by big corporation money.

There are other protestors that are not directly affiliated with a political party but merely protest on a single issue. We recently have the Wall Street protestors comprised of citizens that are becoming aware of the fact that the top executives of Wall Street firms are manipulating large amounts of money in such a way that is economically and morally wrong and is severely undermining the working class economy. The protestors oppose corporate greed and the inequality of our economic system. Politicians label this as class warfare, but it actually is just the working class identifying big business investors as their enemy and starting to fight back after years of redistribution of the wealth from the poor to the rich.

We also have the protestors for amnesty for illegal immigrants who used to wave Mexican flags, but you don't see many of them anymore. We gave them benefits they couldn't get in Mexico and now they are protesting for their rights to more benefits. The working class who pay for these illegal immigrant benefits do not protest on this issue because they have too many more critical complaints against our government and some of them are also controlled indirectly by big corporation money. We more recently had protestor rallies against the State of Wisconsin Republicans who were trying to pass a bill to get rid of the labor unions for government employees and were eventually successful, as was the Republican governor of Ohio. The Republican governors of many other states are trying to repeat this same program in an effort to defeat the labor unions and the other party while gaining financial support from big business. I believe that the labor unions are doing a job that The National Labor Relations Board should have been assigned to perform. However, it seems that currently the only means of fighting big business exploitation of the workers is to join a labor union. The really best way for big businesses to fight the labor unions is to send the best jobs overseas and diminish labor unions and increase business profits at the same time. Labor unions try to help the Democrats financially, like big corporations are primarily helping the Republicans, but their donations are only a drop in the bucket compared to all of the big corporations.

The cost to citizens for the operation of political parties is huge and all the working class gets is gridlock on all economic and campaign affected issues and the promotion of corporate welfare, instead of the general welfare as required by our Constitution. One good example is the failure to change the existing law that anyone born In this country automatically is awarded citizenship We cannot afford to give these benefits to visitors to the United States. All members of Congress realize that this law, established by the Constitution, has now become destructive and should be stopped, but party politics prevents any cooperative action.

If one party tries to accomplish this, the other party must oppose it to prevent any successful legislation "by the enemy." The party that attempts this change will lose the Latino vote as well as the financial support of big corporations that thrive on cheap labor that visits the U.S. legally or illegally. If the members of Congress voted independently and were not bound to a political party or corporate money an amendment to the Constitution could be achieved. The existence of political parties in this country is detrimental to the working class and serves only the desires of the politicians, the political parties and the big corporations that finance them. Instead of strengthening our struggle for democracy in the United States, political parties have slowly eroded it to a point where we no longer have a democratic form of government. We have finally proven the point that we cannot sustain a true democracy if we have political parties and money driving politics.

Most politicians just do what it takes to make more money, even if it is detrimental to the citizens. Whatever party you vote for will not give you any resolution to our major economic problems since Congress is controlled by the big corporations. If we "throw the bums out" the new members will quickly become new bums that accept large campaign contributions and other favors from big corporations. A good portion of this country's wealth is being wasted on politicians and political parties. Instead of proposing to reduce our federal budget by reducing benefits to the working class the Congress should reduce it by eliminating the taxpayer support of politicians and political parties. If no contributions or favors were given to politicians or office holders or contenders and political parties were disbanded, then each American would be an independent voter and Congress and the White House would have to represent the voters rather than big corporations. Taxpayer funds would be used to finance all elections on a fair and equal basis. The political parties and their politicians concentrate their efforts on making money and increasing their power and not on increasing the standard of living of the poor and the working class. Who needs politicians?

In summary of Section 4, politicians and political parties represent a huge financial burden to our economy and, unfortunately, they do very little to benefit the working class, and they help big business investors to exploit the working class citizens. The two political parties often end up in gridlock attempting to knock each other out of office, and so it becomes impossible to pass any legislation to correct our economic disaster. We have gotten to the point where money is electing our government office holders and their efforts are diverted to spending most of their short working hours to campaign funding. Our political system does not promote the general welfare per our Constitution but cashes in on the vulnerability of the working class citizens to get their money and their votes. We have proven the point that we cannot sustain a democracy if we have political parties and money-driven politics.

Section 5. Misleading the Public

How do the big corporations and the politicians mislead the public into believing that they are doing what is in the best interest of the average citizen? They do it by limiting the knowledge of the citizens and influencing them by controlling the news media. This permits them to cover up the fact that the citizens are being exploited to make more money for big business and themselves. In a true democracy the citizens should be able to vote in representatives who would resolve all of these major problems mentioned previously. Unfortunately, the Congress, the White House and the politicians do not represent the average citizens on these major economic issues but do represent the big corporations that give them money and favors. Under our current system of operation in

Congress, the working class would have to give large campaign contributions to the majority of the members of Congress to pass legislation on any of the major economic issues in order to outbid the big corporation contributions. In addition, the working class has not helped with this problem because they have been overwhelmed with big business propaganda regarding our economic difficulties. Most of them will not take any action against big corporations, since they have been trained to dislike big government, rejecting their only means of relief from exploitation by big corporations. Politicians and the news media deliberately confuse the public by concentrating their discussions on the effect of a problem, such as loss of jobs, but avoid discussions on the cause, such as outsourcing our jobs. There has been very little serious discussion concerning these major issues on TV or in other news media which are owned and supported by big businesses. Television and the rest of the news media have no obligation to present the unbiased truth to the public, but follow only the path to greater profits. Television and the entire news media should be owned and operated by an honest government. This would be better for the working-class citizens than Rupert Murdoch owning Fox News; or General Electric, the leader in job outsourcing and corporate tax evasion, owning MSNBC. When TV viewers hear a statement that government and socialism are bad on five different channels on TV it becomes a fact to them. The truth indicates that big government is not bad, but corrupt, inefficient or purchased governments are bad, and governments should actually grow in size to service the additional people and additional problems. Also, socialistic programs like Social Security are not bad for members of the working class because it provides them with more benefits, just as capitalism provides the wealthy business investors with more benefits. Members of the working class must stop being influenced by politicians and big corporation controlled TV programs and support what is best for themselves and other working-class citizens. They must be made to understand that big government, if properly controlled by the citizens is their friend, and many big businesses are currently their enemy.

The standard of living of the middle class has been going down for the past ten years with no prospect of ever obtaining prosperity. The reason for this is that big business investors who control the Congress and the White House through contributions and favors are free to replace American workers with cheaper foreign workers, avoid regulation of financial and commercial businesses, trade with $2/hr. countries, and the list goes on. Many working-class citizens are satisfied with this exploitation because they are living well, but many of them are suffering financially, and some have been actually convinced that government help is destructive to them.

It is unfortunate that big business investors have been able to convince many of the working class citizens that they should oppose any actions by the government to help them because, according to most politicians and news commentators "big government is bad." In reality, government is the only means of stopping big business investors from exploiting the working class. One of our main problems is that the working class is misinformed concerning who is hurting them, It is big business, not big government. Citizens should figure it out by themselves and not be influenced by money-making politicians or the news media. One of the most important functions of a good government is to protect its working citizens from being exploited by the greed of big business, and the lack of this protection is the cause of our current working-class economic disaster.

A lot of politicians and their followers have talked about the negative attributes of a big government. This idea has been initiated by the Republicans and repeated by many Democrats who want to justify campaign contributions received and claim to save the citizens from the abuses of big government like high taxes, regulation, wasteful spending on entitlements and progressive taxation. Some say that government can't do anything right, but we rarely are told when big business makes mistakes because the consumer quietly pays the bill. This is ironical, we have all of the huge problems with our government described in this manuscript and if you turn on your television you get hours of discussion concerning the fight between the two political parties about how much to cut spending. The word "spending" could mean benefits for the working class or taxes for the big businesses, depending on which party you are talking to, but they prefer to generalize to cloud the issue. Our financial deficit problem should not and cannot be resolved by only decreasing spending. We must resolve the problem by also increasing our tax revenues with a new program of manufacturing and selling products within our own country and increasing taxes on corporations from the current 35% back closer to a previous higher numbers from 70% to 90%. With this "spending cuts" bickering politicians and the news media are diverting our attention from the major problems that have damaged our economy.

In the past, there had always been some restrictions on the size and monopolistic tendencies permitted by big corporations. A number of years ago the government forced AT&T to split up because they had a monopoly in the telephone communications industry. This worked out very well and competition was introduced where there was none. However, in the last ten years many restrictions have been removed. For instance, in the area of television programs, they used to limit the number of stations one individual or company could control so the public doesn't get overwhelmingly influenced by a single owner of multiple TV channels. In the past ten years these restrictions have been removed. They should be reduced to only one station per company. Now when a TV viewer hears the same thing on several different channels it becomes a fact in his or her mind. This is how they have created political dirty words such as big government, socialism, spending, labor unions, protectionism (tariffs)" etc. In Sweden "socialism" is not a political dirty word. They favor socialism, and according to a survey their working class ended up being healthier, wealthier, happier and they live longer than the working class in the United States. The form of government we need is a democracy combined with socialism for the basic necessities of life that cannot be trusted to profit-making businesses.

The Constitution has been misrepresented many times and in many ways to satisfy the objectives of individuals and companies seeking to make money any way they can. The Constitution was written over two hundred years ago to satisfy the needs of the citizens at that time and an attempt to also satisfy the needs of future generations as best they could. As time progresses, the needs of the citizens change as indicated by the twenty-six amendments and the continuing need for more changes, many of which are still pending. The creators of the Constitution did an excellent job, but currently there are many important issues they did not cover. So what do the politicians do about this problem? Why, they interpret the Constitution as suits their greedy needs. If you want to fulfill an obligation required for your appointment to the United States Supreme Court you could identify a campaign contribution bribe as a form of free speech. Or you could select a new President of the United States by defining an election system as unfair to one side and then making it unfair to the other side. The voting system in Florida provides for recounts. The Democratic Party asked for a recount in a few counties in year 2000 and the Republican Party did not request any recounts. They could have offered the Republican Party recounts but chose to just deny them to the Democratic Party. A recent decision by the United

States Supreme Court is very troubling. They ruled that a religious group had the right to protest at the burial of a soldier based on the free speech amendment to the Constitution. They should never have considered this case because it is covered well by the laws and the courts. It is against the law to interrupt the privacy of a group of people at a funeral and people should still be held responsible for saying the wrong things at the wrong time. It appears that the United States Supreme Court used this incident to fortify their previous bad decisions concerning free speech, to strengthen their position. Members of The United States Supreme Court should not be appointed by a politician or a political party, but should be elected by popular vote in some non-political group like The National Lawyers Association, or by the citizens.

The National Rifle Association spends a lot of money protecting citizens' rights to have guns. They rally the gun owners and get their money by telling them that the government will take away all of their rifles and guns, which is certainly not true. Some legislators want to outlaw the sale of automatic weapons that are designed to kill people with a deluge of bullets. The Constitution gives the militia the right to bear arms but there were not any automatic weapons at that time so they are not covered. Politicians and businesses interpret the Constitution to fit their own needs to make money. The Constitution is well constructed, but it should not be the final word. What is best for the average citizen at this time in history should be the final word.

The Whitehouse and the CIA could also mislead the public to help them attain their political goals. One possible example of this is the reported assassination of Osama bin Laden. The discussions of the killing of Osama bin Laden in the news media just don't make sense because certain basic information required to tie it all together has been omitted. Here is a list of what I believe is missing.

1. Real pictures (not automated) of the event concerning helicopter landings, entrance to the housing structure and the killing of four occupants. (The seals wore head cameras.)

2. Detailed statements by the navy seals on television describing the attack and explaining why they had to kill unarmed people.

3. The body of Osama bin Laden as uncontested evidence of his death, rather then dumping it into the sea.

4. An explanation of why bin Laden was residing in a conspicuous large fortified compound vulnerable to drone missiles and without armed guards to protect the leader of al-Qaida.

5. A single clean precise description of the series of events concerning the attack instead of the many incorrect statements that had to be later revised.

6. The taking of the DNA samples by an independent trained technician and the use of an independent laboratory in the U.S. to analyze the DNA.

7. The release of the photographs of bin Laden that would give people some visual proof of his death.

8. The verification of the critical proof of bin Laden's death by more than just a small group of CIA members and Navy Seals.

9. Strong opposition by the Republican Party to tear apart the unstable report of the assassination. (What did they get to not contest a successful political action by the other party?)

The only logical explanation that I can think of is that the navy seals killed the wrong people and had to cover up their mistake. The use of polygraph tests on the personnel involved would clear up all of these unanswered questions.

If the working-class citizens accept the principles put forth in this book they can defeat the political propaganda that has plagued them

In summary of Section 5, it is surprising that big business investors and our politicians can successfully deceive the citizens into believing that these people are helping them rather than exploiting them toward poverty. Money controls the news media and especially TV, and when viewers hear the same false information on multiple TV channels it becomes a fact to them. Big corporation money also influences the White House and Congress so they do not engage in serious discussions about outsourcing jobs, lack of business regulations, trading with $2/hr. labor countries, etc. Citizens have been influenced to believe that big government and socialistic programs are bad for the citizens, even though the opposite is actually the truth. Our current corrupt government and attempts to reduce social programs like Social Security are devastating to the working class. Even the United States Supreme Court informs the citizens that giving large campaign contributions to the White House and Congress is a form of free speech (not a bribe).

Section 6. What Are Congress and

The White House Doing to

Correct Our Government?

Most members of Congress don't concentrate their primary efforts on correcting our government but give priority to doing what is required to continue to receive campaign contributions and other favors from big corporations. They actually do not represent the citizens that voted them into office so we have a repeat of one of the primary causes of the Revolutionary War with England, taxation without representation. Besides the problem with our members of Congress promoting the corporate welfare instead of the general welfare per the Constitution, we have the contest between the two major political parties where the rule is to defeat any legislation by the other party so they can be pushed out of office in the next election. Then they always say that the other party should compromise to obtain the necessary votes to pass legislation. This means we end up getting a watered down bill that is of no real value to the working class. One example of this is President Obama's offer to agree to some reductions to Medicare spending as a compromise to get the Republicans to agree to the recent budget deadlock crisis. He was willing to "cut a deal" that would be very harmful to the working-class citizens. Another good example of compromising is the bill that was recently passed on health care. In order to get the required number of votes in the Senate, President Obama agreed to give up the best part of the bill which was the public option for government controlled health care. This meant that he offered no real change because it was still health care insurance and not a government health care program, which costs half the price of our health care insurance program and would get us out of our current position of about thirty seventh in health service value in the world. He added some benefits that were needed like coverage for thirty million people that couldn't afford the insurance, coverage for people with a pre-existing health problem, no cancellation of severely ill members and coverage for children up to twenty six years age. These are good benefits, but the other members would have to pay for them because the HMOs are free to raise prices whenever they desire. So we end up with the same health care insurance we had before with some new benefits that will increase prices for everyone. Forcing some people to purchase health care insurance is wonderful for the HMOs, as if they wrote the health care bill themselves. All we know for sure is that President Obama met with one of the HMO executives six times and the bill is a boon to the HMO industry. I would rather he met with Jim Hightower, Matt Taibbi, Robert Kuttner or Wendell Potter, all of whom have excellent reputations on the study of our health care problem from the working-class perspective. Now the House of Representatives is trying to reject the health care bill that was passed not because it was wrong for the citizens, which it was, but because you don't let the opposition pass any important bills and get credit for it. I would bet my money that if the Republicans were in control of both houses of Congress they would have passed about the same bill as requested by the HMOs. The sad part about this situation is that neither party wants to pass a health care bill to benefit the working class because that would put then in bad standing with the big corporation donors. This certainly calls for a change in the basic objectives of the operation of our government.

Through the years the Senate has established rules of operation that prevent them from serving the citizens correctly and allow the members to obtain more political power. One of these rules is the right to filibuster and prevent the passage of a bill. This means, in effect, instead of big corporations paying a majority of members to stop a bill they might be able to pay only one member. It also means that of all of the members that accept campaign contributions only one has to be exceptionally greedy and stop a bill for his or her financial advantage. There is another rule that is almost unbelievable and that is the requirement of sixty votes for passage of a bill in the Senate. The majority rule philosophy has been suspended, but neither party wants to change it because it currently gives each member supreme authority to stop a bill to justify the receipt of campaign contributions or some other gift. Of course, this ploy can be used to prevent the other party from passing legislation successfully and getting votes. Thus if the Senate is split without a sixty vote majority it is prevented from passing any contested bills, so it currently is not in a good position to resolve any of our major economic problems.

Neither the White House nor the Congress have a desire to directly attack the problem of the loss of millions of jobs in the United States. Neither has delved into a lengthy discussion concerning the jobs that were outsourced to foreign countries, given to foreign worker visa programs, squandered on unfair trade agreements like NAFTA, transferred to foreign countries that offer $2/hr. labor costs, lost through illegal immigration, etc. Many of these were high paying permanent manufacturing and administrative jobs that this country must have to obtain a decent standard of living for the working class. Unlike other recessions, these jobs are not coming back. Even if the demand for goods increases, this need will be filled by foreign workers here or in other countries because of the greed of big business investors. Manufacturing plants are still being moved to Mexico, China, Taiwan and other countries at an alarming rate so we know that things are not going to get better unless we change our course.

The Administration's stimulus programs are not an effective way of creating new jobs. If you give businesses money they will put it in a financial investment program, but they will not just hire more people without an increase in demand for their products or services. I have heard several business owners make this statement on TV and elsewhere. Stimulus money just gives politicians an opportunity to score points with business owners and probably get more campaign contributions and other favors. This inappropriate solution to a major problem was initiated by the Bush Administration and repeated by the Obama Administration. This provided a political football for the politicians and the political parties. They appeared to be working hard for their parties and it allowed them to avoid working on our real economic problems needed by the citizens.

We should look at what the two parties have done to fix our government when they had control of the government through the White House and the Congress. The Bush Administration did not do anything to fix our government when they were in complete control of the administration of the federal government. With their selection of Dick Cheney as Vice President, it was obvious that big business was going to get a lot of concessions. This included large tax breaks, subsidies and the complete freedom to exploit the working class through reducing regulations and not enforcing existing regulations. This permitted them to do things like replacement of American workers with cheaper foreign workers, etc. As a result, our federal budget was changed from a surplus to a huge deficit. They initiated the stimulus program concept with negative results. They continued their efforts for further tax cuts for the wealthy, which got them lots of campaign contributions and votes but, of course, degraded the financial status of the working class.

Another concession to big business was to invade Iraq with the incorrect notion that Iraq had weapons of mass destruction with which to threaten us. By some coincidence, Dick Cheney's old company, Haliburton, received the lion's share of the no-bid contracts. Trillions of dollars were spent in Iraq, but the real loss was that of our young soldiers and no one can tell you for what, other than for big business profits. So the

Republican Party under George Bush did nothing to fix our government but did a lot of things to corrupt the government and reduce the standard of living of the working class and the poor.

Now we look at what the Democrats have done to fix our government. Again, the answer is, nothing to upgrade our poor economy. Both the White House and the Congress have made a choice. They would rather stay in office and make more money than tackle the problems of corruption, the economy, a money-driven form of government, etc. President Obama based his campaign for that office on a slogan "Change You Can Believe In," but people can't believe in it anymore because it never happened. On all major economic issues this Administration had done just about the same as what the Bush Administration would have done. The reason for this is that neither administration or party can do what is best for the working class because big corporation money is in control of most major government economic decisions. President Obama continued the Republican stimulus program and the Wall Street bailout program. He kept key members of the Bush Administration that were definitely anti-working class. When he dropped the public option program in the health care proposal, that was the indicator of the direction in which he was going. Rather than fight for a government controlled health care system, he took the easy choice of an insurance company-controlled system which has already been proven to be a failure for the working class.

In summary of Section 6, the members of Congress and the White House are not primarily promoting the general welfare but are going along with the big business investors in order to obtain large campaign contributions and other favors.

They do not primarily represent the voters that put them in office, so we end up with another situation of "taxation without representation". An example of this is the removal of the "public option" from the health care bill to appease the HMO insurance companies. The Senate also utilizes their filibuster and sixty vote majority rules to prevent any bills from being passed to help the working class. Neither the Congress or the White House seriously takes on the problems of outsourcing jobs, trading with $2/hr. labor countries, unfair trade agreements, relocating manufacturing companies, etc. The stimulus programs did not create sufficient permanent jobs, and the tax cuts sure did not. The primary efforts of both political parties are directed toward defeating the opposition, not helping the working class.

Section 7. What is the Solution

To All of This?

This is a listing of the faults of our government that were discussed and verified in all of the previous discussions and need to be resolved in this section.

1. Big business money is running our government on all major economic issues by the use of bribes, favors and corruption.

2. Many big corporations have given large contributions to politicians and office holders to permit them to continue to exploit the working class-citizens by outsourcing jobs, etc.

3. Lobbyists represent the big corporations in their negotiations with members of Congress and other office holders regarding campaign contributions and other favors offered to the members.

4.Our form of government has changed from a democracy (ruled by the ruled) to a plutocracy (ruled by money).

5. Most politicians do not represent the working class citizens but primarily represent the big corporations that give them money and other favors.

6. Political parties take the individual votes away from the private citizens and utilize them as a block of votes to satisfy their own desires for power and financial gain.

7. Political parties will prefer gridlock instead of reform rather than allow the other party to pass any successful bills.

8. The White House, The Congress, The United States Supreme Court, The Judiciary Courts and the state and local governments are all promoting the corporate welfare instead of the general welfare as required by our Constitution.

9. A good portion of our economic activities are being completely wasted by occupations that are of no productive value and are destructive to the working class in this country. Examples of these unproductive middleman money manipulator occupations are politicians, political parties, Wall Street, future traders, lobbyists, investment brokers and anyone that creates money by speculating or gambling with someone else's money.

10. The news media and especially television are controlled by big corporation money and prevented from engaging in serious discussions concerning the failure of our government to promote the general welfare in areas like replacing American workers with cheaper foreign workers, trading with $2/hr. countries, money driven politics, etc. The working class is being misled so they have not taken any combined action to correct our government problems.

11. The political agenda of the working class has been sidetracked by politicians, political parties and big corporation money to the extent that protestors carry signs rejecting big government and socialism, their only paths to prosperity.

12. The working class possesses only 4% of the nation's wealth, which is morally and economically unacceptable.

13. Both political parties cooperate with big corporations to obtain campaign contributions and other favors, but the Republican Party usually gets eighty percent of the money because they go all out by proposing no regulation of businesses, spending cuts to working class benefits and tax cuts only for the wealthy.

14. Inflation and prices no longer increase gradually as they used to, but they increase in large jumps continuously, and there is considerable price gouging.

15. Trading with communistic dictatorships like China increased their financial strength so they may someday surpass our power and

challenge the United States.

16. Politicians have managed to stop the enforcement of our illegal immigration laws which has placed a financial burden on the working class who compete with illegal immigrants for jobs and social benefits.

17. Our move to global trading and the World Trade Organization with their $2/hr. labor has cost us millions of our best paying jobs, huge trading deficits and a devastated economy for the working class.

18. Oil and gasoline prices are increased on a regular basis by futures traders and refineries and need to be stabilized by our government, even if they have to take over this critical industry.

19. Giving subsidies to businesses is senseless and should be discontinued. We should only give loans to critical businesses that cannot survive.

20. Deceit is used in this country extensively to exploit and devastate the working class citizens and the failure to employ polygraph lie detectors has resulted in the loss of billions of dollars in the operation of police stations, courts, businesses, government, crime, drug abuse and many other activities.

All twenty of these government faults could be condensed into one simple statement. Big corporations exploiting the public, unproductive occupations and the greed of politicians and middleman money- manipulators are financially ruining our country.

We have all of these important issues that require immediate attention but the Congress wasted its time by fighting over avoiding a debt default that was threatened by the Republicans. They then insisted that we reduce the deficit by decreasing the benefits to the working class. The correct solution would have been to vote on just raising the debt limit and let the voters see which Congress members voted for a financial catastrophe. However, the Republicans preferred gridlock so they could obtain credit for promoting corporate welfare. This further proves that the basic concept of our political system must be changed.

All of the activities that our government is doing incorrectly that have been described above set up a pattern concerning the primary single factor that is the cause of all of this corruption and business activity that is damaging to the working class. What is at the foundation of all of this is that money has taken control of our government and we must stop this activity and change our current plutocracy to a truly democratic form of government. We have proven that a democratic form of government cannot survive if money is permitted to influence our office holders.

To resolve these problems we must make drastic changes in the way our government operates, but this cannot be done as long as big corporation money controls the Congress and the White House. This could be accomplished if the working class citizens would act together to attain this difficult goal. They comprise a majority of the population and if they all work together in the right direction they can fix our decayed government. Many of them still have their jobs and are surviving by working in the service industries or holding multiple poor paying jobs. They have a tendency to think that even though millions have lost their jobs, they personally are surviving satisfactorily. They should consider that sending jobs and entire industries overseas will make the competition greater for the remaining good jobs and the job situation will be worsening so they could lose their jobs sometime in the future. They should also want to upgrade the standard of living for the working class in general for a better future for all of them. Citizens should make an effort to help the working class and the poor even if they are surviving this financial catastrophe.

I recommend four major initial steps to fixing our government the first of which is to remove all of the false information placed in the minds of many working class citizens by politicians as directed by big business money. We must convince the working class and the poor in this country to realize just what the money-makers have been doing to deny them the prosperity that is entitled to them if they put forth their efforts in the right direction. This book will provide the basis to get them started but they have a long way to go to really understand what has been accomplished by the big corporations, the politicians, the lobbyists, the Congress, the White House, Wall Street and all of the middlemen money-manipulators to reduce the standard of living of the citizens, many of whom are hopelessly working hard in a futile attempt to obtain prosperity.

In the second major step the working class citizens must take positive actions to notify the White House and the members of Congress that they want a major change in the way our government operates. One possible approach would be to notify the President and their members of Congress that they will not vote in any elections until the Congress passes complete campaign finance reform where all campaign expenses are funded by the taxpayers. It would certainly help if the citizens participated in demonstrations all around the country and especially in Washington D.C. This could be accomplished if the working class citizens could be induced to act together to attain this difficult but essential goal.

Once the majority of our citizens agree to take on the job of changing our form of government, the root problem of big corporations giving campaign contributions and other favors to the members of Congress and the White House must be resolved before they can go any further. In this third major step it will be very difficult to get the Congress to pass the legislation to fix our government because most of the members are firmly tied into the desires of big corporation money. There is another possible approach to force the Congress to fix our corrupt government. Members of Congress claim that they are not influenced by the money and favors given to them by big corporations. Working-class citizens should contact the President and insist that he issue an executive order declaring that the use of polygraph testing will be expanded for government employees starting with the members of Congress. Just the thought of lie detection testing will bring the members of Congress in line and stop a lot of corruption in our government. The testing could later be expanded in state and city governments. It is an excellent means of resolving the problems of deceit in government and business that have been costing the citizens dearly through the years. The President could further perfect polygraph testing (though it is sufficiently perfected to be use now) and the newer speech stress lie detecting system.

If the President won't take on the polygraph promotion job then a fourth major step should be taken in the form of ballot proposition petitions in all states, declaring that the money should be taken out of politics by establishing a program of paying for all political campaigns only with taxpayer money. Unfortunately, ballot propositions are not permitted in federal elections.

There are many other steps that must be subsequently taken. The allegiance of voters to political parties must be stopped. Political parties thrive on money from businesses and individual citizens and are one of the major causes of the corruption in our government. They represent their financial supporters and not the citizens of this country. Most of their efforts are directed toward defeating the other party with little regard, if any, for the well being of the voters. Neither political party will ever voluntarily assist the working class concerning major economic issues because they would have to forfeit big corporation money. This has been proven by the fact that the current Democratic Administration is doing the same thing on major economic issues as the previous Republican Administration. Both political parties will certainly fight to the bitter end to prevent taking the money out of politics. We should engage in a program to lead voters into a new system of one hundred percent independent voters, and I don't mean for them to join the current Independent Voter Party, but to remain independent of any party. In order to have a true democratic form of government people cannot be banded in groups with leaders who want to do things their way which usually is to make money for themselves. The working-class citizen must think of his or her own requirements and not let party leaders decide what is best for them. As long as you have political parties it will make it almost impossible to take the money out of politics and get rid of the uncontrolled corruption.

We must set aside the notion that businesses create most of the jobs and provide financial incomes for millions of the citizens so let them operate with the single goal of increasing their profits. We must replace it with the notion that the main purpose of businesses in the United States is to provide the workers with permanent jobs with good working conditions that provide a living wage wherever possible and to make a fair profit to sustain their existence. All businesses should be notified that if they want to operate within the United States they must abide by a new set of very strict rules that prevent them from exploiting the working class. It should be made known that big corporations are not individuals as indicated by the United States Supreme Court. They certainly are not humane, being overseen by a board of directors that has a single goal of increasing profits at any cost. If this arrangement is unacceptable to any businesses they should be directed to cease operations in the United States. This would not be that great of a loss because these would be the businesses that have avoided employing American workers whenever possible. This is called promoting the general welfare in accordance with our Constitution and avoiding the current practice of promoting the corporate welfare.

After completing the initial step of changing our form of government from our current plutocracy (rule by money) to a true democracy (rule by the ruled) then we can take on the job of further correcting all of the corruption and inconsistencies discussed previously. Without changing our form of government we could never even attempt to clean up this mess because of the power of money in politics, the aggressive fighting between our two major political parties and the Senate rules of filibustering and a sixty vote super majority which could make it inoperable on major contested issues. So another important step in this government fixing procedure would be to strike down the filibuster and sixty vote rules in Congress. Our current system of government has not been constructed to be able to resolve our large volume of problems and through the years it has evolved into groups of people that have devised a means of making money without performing a useful service to our society and consequently destroying the value of our society.

Foreign worker visa programs should be completely eliminated. If businesses cannot find sufficient workers with the right training they will have to train them. All foreign trade agreements should be reviewed and the unfair activities removed, like NAFTA and China's 25 % tariff on U.S. cars sold there. All parts for cars should be manufactured in the United States as well as the final assembly. The United States immigration laws should be enforced and strengthened and the border fences completed. Companies should be penalized for hiring illegal immigrants and required to check their legal status prior to all hiring. All benefits currently given to illegal immigrants should eventually be discontinued with the exception of emergency health services. Politicians are quick to casually state that we can't send them back to Mexico. This is just not true, and don't think that it would cost too much because we would save billions of dollars spent each year supporting them. However, if we stop giving them jobs it is likely that most of them would go back to Mexico the same way as they came here, on their own.

Banks and other financial institutions should be strictly regulated to prevent them from exploiting the public. There should be a maximum interest rate of around 7% like it used to be years ago. Banks should be restricted to a leverage of 10% of capital on loans and even eliminate the leverage completely if possible. Customers should not be sold mortgages they cannot afford and mortgages should not be bundled and sold overseas. Banks should not engage in speculation. Wall Street should be strictly regulated and any practices that harm the working class removed. There should be absolutely no gambling on investments like the current derivatives and swaps. The possibility of completely eliminating Wall Street operations should be investigated, including the feasibility of making it a government controlled business where the taxpayers get any huge profits that may still exist.

Trading on future products should be completely eliminated based on the fact that traders do not take delivery to perform legitimate hedging and are merely increasing prices and inflation, which are both devastating to the working class. Those big hedging funds are not hedging at all, but the word "hedging" is their key to deceiving the public into thinking they are hedging and performing an actual business function instead of just speculating for money. Financial businesses should be confined to commercial transactions and not speculation and gambling with someone else's money. Price gouging should be stopped. The new Consumer Protection Agency being held up by Republicans should be activated and get involved in identifying price-gouging situations. Eventually it might be possible to fix prices on all products and services including real estate, and reduce inflation down to a minimum. The millions of unproductive occupations in this country should be eliminated including politicians, political parties, future traders, investment institutions and all money manipulators.

The Federal Reserve System should not be allowed to cut interest rates to near zero to stimulate business during a recession because it destroys a source of income for senior citizens and others and creates inflation, but does not increase jobs, They know it, but won't admit that only increases in demand can justify increasing jobs

. Corporations that are too big to fail should be reduced in size and be divested of all monopolistic tendencies. Consolidation of big businesses should be discouraged. Foreign investments should be restricted and investments within the United States promoted. The TV industry should be completely revised with a rule restricting the ownership of channels to one, as well as the ownership of all forms of the news media. Government ownership of TV channels should be investigated.

At a time of economic stress our financial resources and American lives are wasted by our involvement in Iraq and Afghanistan and maintaining a presence in many other countries for no worthwhile reason other than making money for politicians and big businesses with no-bid contracts, including Haliburton and thousands of other big corporations. It has been verified that the reason for invading Iraq was invalid because there were no weapons of mass destruction in Iraq. We should withdraw our forces from Afghanistan immediately, because nothing we could accomplish there is worth the loss of another American life and the financial costs. We should also withdraw all of our forces currently in Germany, Korea, Japan, Bosnia and anywhere else they have been incorrectly placed for the financial convenience of politicians and big corporations.

One of the ways that the big corporations and their associated politicians are able to promote the corporate welfare instead of the general welfare and get away with it is through deceit. The Republican Party can try to deny critical benefits like Social Security to the working class and still get working class citizens to vote for them. The Democrats can propose amnesty for illegal immigrants that would severely damage the working class economy, but working class citizens still vote for them. Businesses, politicians and criminals fleece the public through deceit and all of our lives are made difficult by this deceit. We have the means of eradicating most of this devastating deceit but fail to use it because the deceivers are in control of our government and the propaganda media. The polygraph lie detector is currently an available means of determining if a person is lying. Of course, there is strong opposition against its use by most politicians, courts, government office holders, businesses executives and just plain citizens, so its use is opposed and many dollars have been spent to falsely label it as unreliable. However, it has been scientifically proven to be reliable enough to get the job done. A study of the polygraph conducted by the Royal Canadian Mounted Police revealed that it was 100% accurate on suspects who failed the test, because they were later confirmed guilty by a trial. The polygraph was inaccurate on 10% of the suspects who passed the test and were later confirmed guilty. This means that 10% of all polygraph participants could possibly get away with not being detected, but no one will be accused unfairly. Those that failed the polygraph test could be immediately sentenced by a judge and those that passed could be sent to trial if the evidence against them was overwhelming. This is a better record than the courts and certainly proves the use of the polygraph to be an effective method of weeding out liars. O.J. Simpson failed a polygraph test regarding the killing of his wife, but a jury with emotional members set him free. Another emotional jury set Casey Anthony free, but a polygraph test would have convicted her of an obvious criminal action and save the state three years of needless financial expenditure plus a failure of justice. Another way of looking at the polygraph's reliability would be to say that all of the participants that failed were lying, and 10% of the participants beat the machine, but they could be further investigated or sent to trial. The expansion of the use of polygraph testing would afford an excellent means of investigating politicians and government office holders for corruption, but the tests must be conducted by reliable individuals such as those accepted by the National Polygraph Association. In southern California anyone can buy a machine and go into business. This lack of proper regulation gives the polygraph a bad reputation, which politicians like. The expansion of the use of the polygraph in government, business and society would greatly enhance the living conditions of the working class.

A summary of Section 7 stating all of the above suggestions about how to accomplish our goals is listed below.

1. Get all of the working class citizens to realize that they are being exploited by big corporations and the politicians, the lobbyists, the Congress, the White House, Wall Street and all of the middleman money manipulators.

2. Notify the White House, the Congress and everyone that we want complete campaign finance reform to take the money out of politics and we won't vote again until we get it.

3. Expand the use of the polygraph starting with the members of Congress to prove that campaign contributions are actually bribes, and then cover the police, the courts, etc.

4. If other attempts have failed, initiate ballot propositions in all of the states to obtain complete campaign contribution reform and to expand the use of polygraph testing to Congress and other government employees.

5. Initiate a program of requiring all citizens to

vote independently and eliminate all political parties.

6. Enforce the proposition that the purpose of business in the U,S. is to provide the workers with good paying permanent jobs and not just to provide businesses with maximum profits.

7. Change the many damaging rules like filibustering, sixty vote super majority and citizenship for babies born to visitors to the U.S.

8. Cease the current practice of replacing American workers with cheaper foreign Workers. This includes discontinuing trading with $2/hr. foreign labor countries, returning manufacturing plants and out-sourced jobs to the U.S., cancellation of all foreign-worker visa programs and correcting all unfair trade agreements.

9. Discontinue all benefits given to illegal immigrants other than emergency health care, enforce current illegal immigration laws and force businesses to verify the citizenship of employees.

10. Strictly regulate all businesses by enforcing 7% maximum interest rates and 3% minimum and the elimination of all middlemen money manipulation activities.

11. Discontinue the current practice of using our armed forces to intervene in civil wars in other countries just to provide lucrative no-bid contracts to big corporations.

12. Initiate a government program of redistribution of the wealth from the big business investors to working-class citizens who own only 4% of

the nation's wealth.   Start by reducing the
taxes on the working class drastically and
and increasing the taxes on the wealthy
drastically.

13. Reverse our current government programs of
promoting the corporate welfare to promoting
the general welfare to comply with our
Constitution.

14. Force the members of Congress to represent
the citizens that voted them into office and
stop the exploitation of the working class by
big business investors.

15. Install a form of government that is a
democracy combined with socialism for the basic
necessities of life that cannot be trusted to profit-
making businesses.

Our government was originally established as a republic by the Declaration of Independence, later structured as a democracy by The Constitution of The United States, decimated through the years by the money-makers and changed to a plutocracy and now needs to be changed back to a democracy. The primary cause of the current economic devastation of the working class is their exploitation by big business investors with the help of the politicians, lobbyists and office holders. The only way to bring prosperity to the working class is to install complete campaign finance reform where all campaigns are paid for by the taxpayers and to manufacture and sell products within the United States.

Section 8. Previous Letters Concerning

Our Government Faults

Listed below are the letters that I submitted to the local newspapers for publishing over the past years. The information stated previously was primarily based on these articles. Reading this will provide a little different approach to the subject and also some new details.

Is It Good for the Stock Market?

A group of news analysts on Fox News were discussing the various bills that could be considered by the new Congress. A first question that was usually asked was:" Will it be good for the stock market? " Years back, the predominant question used to be: " Will it be good for the citizens? "

Under our present global economy, what is good for the investment economy is usually bad for the working economy. The reason for this change, of course, is that the number one method of competing in our global economy is to replace American labor with cheaper foreign labor. There is no way that over $20/hour American labor can compete with less than $2/hour foreign labor.

Fox News is promoting corporate welfare rather than the general welfare as stated in our Constitution. You know that something is wrong when they have to continually advertise that they are "fair and balanced". They lead the news commentators in misleading the public.

Occupations Without Value

It is conceivable that over half of this country's citizens are engaged in occupations that are not creating anything of value to the average citizen. They are involved in businesses that manipulate money as middlemen for financial transactions, such as future traders, investment brokers, banks involved in speculation and Wall Street financiers. If you want to make big money these days you place yourself between someone that has something of value to sell and someone who desires to purchase that item, then you just take your cut of the transaction. Distributors are middlemen that perform an actual service, but since no one seems to be promoting the general welfare anymore many of them have resorted to price gouging to increase their profits. Farmers complain that they received half of what they received for potatoes last year, and the consumers are paying four times what they paid last year. This giving "government printing presses" to businesses has resulted in severe inflation which is devastating to the working class. My retirement money isn't worth one tenth of what it was when I retired.

A Wakeup Call for the Working Class

Most people know that the political decisions regarding our economy are controlled by big business investor money because of the current programs of replacing American workers with foreign workers, big tax cuts for the wealthy, lack of business regulation, etc. The only way to stop this corruption of our government is for the members of the working class to all work together to change our form of government from our current plutocracy (ruled by money) to a democracy (ruled by the ruled). Many member of the working class are surviving this economic disaster, but if they don't oppose the politicians and big corporation money now, they could be sorry later when they are eventually financially devastated. You should constantly notify your members of Congress that you want to take the money out of politics so they can represent the citizens rather than the big corporations. The Wall Street protestors have recognized the resulting unequal distribution of the wealth in this country and are putting forth an effort to get it changed. Don't expect the politicians and office holders to relieve our corruption problem.

Politicians Always Survive

Because we have political parties politicians can say or do most anything they desire to increase their financial and political agendas. If they say something wrong half of the voters in this country will back them up because they belong to the same party. If the Democrats propose amnesty for illegal immigrants or the Republicans propose absolutely no regulation of businesses most of the working class citizens will go along with it and still support that party. I claim that you cannot have a truly democratic form of government if you permit the existence of political parties. To be truly democratic all of the citizens must act and vote independently of any political party.

An example of how politicians survive is the recent reporting of Newt Gingrich earning millions of dollars from mortgage lender Freddie Mac through his consulting firm for advising them not to give loans to people who do not have a good credit history. At the same time the Freddie Mac executives are saying that they have to give their top people huge salaries and bonuses in order to obtain the required exceptional talent to make the correct decisions. But they still need the advice of Newt Gingrich? You or I could have given them that advice for half the price!

Demonstrations Against Wall Street

I have to give the Wall Street protestors credit for being the first large group of protestors to ever chose as their opponent the number one cause of the devastation of the working class economy, which is corporate greed. The Tea Party protestors chose political propaganda items such as "business regulations", "socialism" and "big government", which actually help the working class, but sure do diminish big business investor profits. There are thousands of big corporations in this country that practice corporate greed, but the financial sector is particularly devastating to the working class because they do not offer a product or a service that benefit the average citizen, and generate severe inflation by their questionable money manipulation practices of derivatives, swaps and bidding against their own offerings, plus the periodic threat of a financial market crash. We have permitted them pseudo-government printing presses. We need to completely eliminate all of these destructive Wall Street activities, but first we must take the money out of politics so the members of Congress and the White House will represent the working class citizens instead of big business investors.

Wall Street Protestors vs. Tea Party

The protestors started because the citizens of this country are becoming aware of the fact that the top executives of Wall Street firms are manipulating large amounts of money in such a way that is economically and morally wrong and it is severely undermining the working class economy. The Tea Party was started because the big business investors provided the funds for the Republican Party to initiate a new group to promote ultra-conservative policies that would increase business profits. The protestors oppose corporate greed and government inequality and want to tax Wall Street as a partial solution. (I believe they should try for a complete solution by eliminating all of the Wall Street activities that are devastating the working class economy.) The Tea Party wants to reduce government regulation of businesses so that businesses can continue to exploit the working class citizens by replacing

American workers with cheaper foreign workers.
The protestors believe that big business investors
are the enemy of the working class, while the Tea
Party members believe that big government is the
enemy. (I believe that our government is not
functioning properly not because it is too big, but
because it is completely controlled by big business
money.)

Illegal Immigration Burden
On the Working Class

President Obama was correct when he
stated that giving benefits to the illegal immigrants
was humane. It also gives the Democratic Party a
lot of Hispanic votes. The votes are so important
that the California Legislature passed The Dream

Act to give illegal immigrants financial educational assistance when many citizens are being denied an education because of exorbitant tuition increases, but this was necessary because over half of the residents in California are Hispanic. What the President did not tell us is that permitting illegal immigrants to reside in the United States creates a heavy burden on the working class citizens who must compete with them for education, health care, jobs and welfare. The state of California spends 10.5 billion dollars each year to support these illegal immigrants, which amounts to about $1,200 from each taxpayer. What the President has promoted is not humane for the working class citizens, but obtaining the Hispanic vote is a high priority for his reelection. The President should make an effort to stop illegal immigration by stopping businesses from hiring them and denying them all benefits except emergency health care.

Don't Let Politicians Influence You

If you are a member of the working class you should be very cautious about accepting any information stated by a politician or a government office holder. These people are not promoting the general welfare as per our Constitution, but are promoting the corporate welfare, as they are paid to do by campaign contributions and other favors from big corporations. Citizens should not support politicians and office holders because they are in your political party, but should only support them when they proposing what is advantageous for you and the rest of the working class. These days, the primary goal of a political party is not to do what is best for the average citizen, but to give their highest priority to winning elections. If they don't get into office they do not get large campaign contributions that keep them there, perhaps or life. The way our election system works today, promoting benefits for the working class does not get candidates into office, they need the money.

It sounds hopeless, and it is, if we do not take all of the money out of politics and go back to promoting the general welfare. The change has to start with complete campaign finance reform where the taxpayers pay for all campaigns.

Disappointed With President Obama

I have been voting for the Democratic Party for over twenty-five years because the Republican Party advertises that they want to eliminate Social Security, Medicare, Medicaid and many other benefits received by the working class. They also want to remove the regulation of big business that decreases the exploitation of the working class and they fight for tax breaks for the wealthy. However, both political parties accept large campaign contributions and favors from the big business investors and permit them to replace American workers with cheaper foreign workers and many other devastating economic policies. President Obama has ignored the many campaign promises about major changes to benefit the working class and is traveling the same economic route as President Bush did, as paid for by the big business investors. He immediately dropped the public option in the health care bill, ignoring his earlier promise of a single payer system that could cut the costs in half. His latest reversal of normal Democratic policy was to oppose the smog clean-air regulation that would cost big business up to $90 billion a year, calling it a regulatory burden, like any good Republican would do.

Reviewing 9/11 Charities

There was a recent article in the North County Times concerning investigations regarding some of the charities set up to honor the victims of the 9/11 attack by al-Qaida. One of the numerous charities is a group that are spending $713,000 to create a memorial quilt the size of 25 football fields to honor the victims of 9/11. The relatives of those killed in the airplane crashes are probably all millionaires by now and don't need any financial aid. The relatives of those remaining victims of the building crashes do need financial assistance as do the citizens killed in tornados and other national tragedies. Spending $713,000 to create a memorial quilt that has no practical value is a waste of money that should be given directly to the financially depleted relatives.

As would be expected, the 9/11 attack turned out to be a bonanza for the politicians and some business people who are taking advantage of the public sentiment for the victims. The politicians get the support of the voters and possibly some of the money, and the businesses get the lion's share of the $713,000. Charities are usually run by nonprofit organizations, but the director and his or her relatives could draw excessive salaries and expense accounts. All business activities need more regulation.

The Purpose of Politicians
And Political Parties

Most American citizens have been led to believe that the purpose of politicians and political parties is to assist the voters to select the candidates for public office that will represent their best interests. In reality, they do just the opposite and assist big corporations and the politicians to extract large sums of money from the working class to satisfy their financial greed. The way this system has been working for years is that the big corporations give campaign contributions and favors to the politicians, political parties and federal and state legislators to obtain favorable legislation such as large tax reductions, subsidies and other benefits such as free oil drilling rights. These payoffs are usually done through lobbyists who negotiate the transactions and shield the big corporations from financial wrongdoing. The United States Supreme Court approves of this activity, identifying it as a form of free speech. This system has been devastating to the working class citizens because of the resulting replacement of American workers by foreign workers, lack of regulation of businesses, trading with $2/hr. labor countries, and the list goes on.

The working class will not obtain prosperity until they all vote independently to take the money out of politics with <u>complete</u> campaign finance reform. And yes, all politicians and political parties should be eliminated because they deny prosperity to the working class rather than create it and they certainly do not promote the general welfare per our Constitution.

Evaluating the Dream Act

More politicians are climbing aboard the bandwagon to gain popularity with the Latino voters by promoting passage of The Dream Act.

Unfortunately, what is a sweet dream for some people can be a nightmare for others. Passing a bill to have the taxpayers pay part of the college tuition for illegal immigrants appears to be humane as President Obama has stated, but the average taxpayer cannot afford it, and it is not humane for them. Any taxpayer money that is available should be spent on helping the millions of middle class citizens who are in severe financial trouble because these same politicians permitted big corporations to transfer their jobs to foreign countries. These illegal immigrants have broken our immigration laws by attempting to resolve Mexico's poverty problem by adding a great financial burden to the working class citizens of the United States. Besides this additional college tuition financial burden, the working class citizens are forced to compete with the illegal immigrants for jobs, health care, primary education, food stamps and reductions in wages such as the construction industry going from $21/hr. to $9/hr. This is just another way to promote illegal immigration to the extent that fences can't be built high enough to keep them out even if we enforced our immigration laws.

Proof of the Death of Osama bin Laden

The public has received no actual proof of the recent reported killing of Osama bin Laden. I do not doubt that he is dead, but I do have questions about how and when he died. The report of his death is inconclusive because the DNA sample selection and the testing were performed by a small group of CIA members aboard the aircraft carrier and the body, the uncontested evidence, was dumped into the sea. There was no armed opposition in that room and no need to kill people. Osama bin Laden was shot in the face, which would normally be preserved as evidence of his death. Three of the government officials that saw the photograph of bin Laden did not say that it looked like him, but they all emphatically stated that they were sure he was dead. It is conceivable that they all were informed that he had died prior to this event?

This could all be resolved by a polygraph test of the Navy Seal who shot bin Laden and the CIA member that conducted the DNA sample selection and tests. Polygraph tests are accurate when someone lies, but cannot detect when a person makes a false statement that they believe is true. Unfortunately, polygraph testing is very unpopular with most politicians.

Redistribution of the Wealth

In the world of politics the redistribution of the wealth is considered to be a dirty word. If one politician proposes to increase the federal income taxes for only the wealthy citizens the other one cries "that's redistribution of the wealth" without any explanation, because all of us are supposed to know that it is an unacceptable action. However, a redistribution of the wealth from the poor to the rich has been going on for the past ten years, but that is acceptable if the wealthy are giving large contributions to you and your political party. It is almost inconceivable that two percent of the citizens of this country are holding ninety percent of the wealth. Our politicians tell us that in order to bring prosperity to the working class we must be more competitive when trading with $2/hr. labor countries in the World Trade Organization. This is impossible! We should not trade with $2/hr. labor countries but should manufacture and sell products within the U.S. What the working class needs is a reversal of the current redistribution of the wealth policy on a large scale.

Judicial System Reform

Over many years we have seen that our system of courts is not functioning properly. The jury system has proven to have failed on numerous occasions, including the O.J. Simpson and the Casey Anthony cases. The average citizen serving on a jury is not able to control his or her emotions well enough to hand down a proper verdict. Many countries in Europe and around the world have solved this problem by replacing juries with a panel of three or five trained judges. And, of course, there is the problem of judges being appointed by political parties, to which they may be indebted enough to influence their decisions. Judges should be voted into office by the Bar Association or the citizens.

All of these problems could be resolved by the use of the polygraph lie detector device that would provide accurate judicial decisions at a fraction of the current cost to the taxpayers. Regardless of what the politicians tell you, polygraph tests do correctly detect when someone is lying. It cannot determine when someone believes something to be true that is actually not true, but who cares? There is strong opposition in this country against the extensive use of polygraph testing, and this includes most judges and politicians. It certainly would help the working class citizens. Unfortunately, political parties prefer gridlock rather than reform.

The Wealthy vs. the Working Class

It has been pretty well established that the wealthy investors in this country own about 90% of the wealth while the working class own only about

10%. This is morally and economically wrong and should be corrected. Of course, the big business investors also own the Congress, the politicians and even part of the working class, so the road to correction is not easy. Some say that they are just trying to earn a profit on their investment, but I say that they should not be permitted to earn excessive profits at the expense of the working class by replacing American workers with cheaper foreign workers, purchasing subsidies and tax breaks from the politicians, trading with $2/hr. labor countries, and the list goes on.

The wealthy big business investors should be required to contribute to their obligations to the working class who provided the labor for their financial successes and struggled and some lost their lives to save the investor's assets from being lost to Adolph Hitler in WWII. The working class will never be able to obtain prosperity as long as big business money is permitted to exploit them into poverty.

What is Missing in the
bin Laden Narrative?

The discussions of the killing of Osama bin Laden in the news media just don't make sense because certain basic information required to tie it all together has been omitted. Here is a list of what I believe is missing.

1. Real pictures of the event concerning helicopter landings, entrance to the housing

structure and the killing of some occupants.

2. Detailed statements by the navy seals on television describing the attack and explaining why they had to kill unarmed people.

3. The body of Osama bin Laden as uncontested evidence of his death.

4. An explanation of why bin Laden was residing in a conspicuous large fortified compound vulnerable to drone missiles and without armed guards to protect the leader of al-Qaida.

5. A single clean precise description of the series of events concerning the attack instead of the many incorrect statements that had to be later revised.

6. The taking of the DNA samples by an independent trained technician and the use of an independent laboratory in the U.S. to analyze

the DNA.

7. The release of the photographs of bin Laden that would give people some visual proof of his death.

8. The verification of the critical proof of bin Laden's death by more than just a group of CIA members.

9. Strong opposition by the Republican Party to tear apart the unstable report of the assassination. (What did they get to not contest a successful political action by the other party?)

The Purpose of Politicians
and Political Parties

Most American citizens have been led to believe that the purpose of politicians and political parties is to assist the voters to select the candidates for public office that will represent their best interests. In reality, they do just the opposite and assist big corporations and the politicians to extract large sums of money from the working class to satisfy their financial greed. The way this system has been working for years is that the big corporations give campaign contributions and favors to the politicians, political parties and federal and state legislators to obtain favorable legislation such as large tax reductions, subsidies and other benefits such as free oil drilling rights. These payoffs are usually done through lobbyists who negotiate the transactions and shield the big corporations from financial wrongdoing. The United States Supreme Court approves of this activity, identifying it as a form of free speech. This system has been devastating to the working class citizens because of the resulting replacement of American workers by foreign workers, lack of regulation of businesses, trading with $2/hr. labor countries, and the list goes on.

The working class will not obtain prosperity until they all vote independently to take the money out of politics with complete campaign finance reform. And yes, all politicians and political parties should be eliminated because they deny prosperity to the working class rather than create it and they certainly do not promote the general welfare per our Constitution.

Lack of Action on High

Oil and Gas Prices

President Obama has just appointed a commission to determine whether commodity future traders are the cause of our current high oil and gas prices. About a year or two ago both Houses of Congress investigated the problem and both of them came to the same conclusion that the high prices were caused primarily by the futures traders and not normal supply and demand. Mr. George Soros, one of the individuals that profited three billion dollars in one year by futures trading, confirmed their conclusion. The Senate is hung up on a watered down bill that won't fully resolve the problem. President Obama is a little late with his study proposal, which is probably only an excuse to avoid the problem. It is time for someone in our government to take action to disallow all trading on futures and only allow legitimate hedging where delivery of the product will be accepted. On all major economic issues both of our recent Presidents have taken the actions desired by big corporation money. Welcome to our plutocracy (ruled by money), and goodbye to our democracy (ruled by the ruled). High gas prices are devastating to the working class citizens, but in a plutocracy exploiting the citizens is a high priority. If you are confused by what is going on in our government and politics, just look for who is making the money and it will all become understandable.

The Real Federal Budget Problem

The Republicans want to reduce benefits to the working class like Medicare, Medicaid and Social Security while giving tax cuts to the wealthy citizens. President Obama is interested in cutting a deal and getting credit for avoiding a financial shutdown. The President should say he will have nothing to do with either proposal even if the government shuts down financially. The Republicans have spent money in the Bush Presidency on the war in Iraq, tax cuts and favors for the wealthy big corporations large enough to change our treasury surplus to a huge deficit, but they don't want to spend money for benefits for the working class. The problem here is that both political parties owe allegiance to the big corporations for their large campaign contributions and other favors. Why else would they want to even consider promoting corporate welfare instead of the general welfare as required by the Constitution?

I can think of two ways to reduce the treasury deficit, one is to reduce spending, but only the second, increasing the tax revenues, would be good for the working class. Taxes for the wealthy should be increased to back where they used to be and we should bring back all of the jobs that were sent to foreign countries and then manufacture and sell products within the United States to further increase our tax revenues.

The U.S. World Police Force

They are having a revolt against their dictator in Libya so the President of the United States has an opportunity for decisiveness by assisting the rebels. He says that saving the lives of the people is the humane thing to do. Most of the countries in Africa could use some of this humane assistance and their circumstances are a lot worse than that of the Libyan citizens, with killings and rapes going on continuously. In addition, it is very possible that the replacement regime in Libya could be worse than the current dictatorship, while the poor people in Africa don't harbor global terrorists and are friends of the U.S.

This administration finally found a program that the Republicans would not oppose vigorously, since both political parties gain financial security by supplying big corporations with lucrative no bid contracts. Each missile fired provides one million dollars more in business.

It is harmful to the working class for administrations to attempt to police the world. We lose the money, and more important, it's not worth one of our young soldiers' lives. Let them fight their own civil wars. Even if the United Nations takes over the leadership, who do you think will lose the most soldiers and money?

Expand the Use of the Polygraph

The citizens of this country are being deceived on almost a daily basis and it is hurting them both financially and physically. Members of Congress are supposed to be representing the voters who put them in office, but are they are primarily representing the big corporations that give them large campaign contributions and other favors. Are all of the judges in our courts completely unbiased in handing down their decisions? Are politicians and the news media truthful in their comments concerning the real cause of our poor economy? Are Wall Street and other investment brokers being fair to the public when they manipulate investments? And the list goes on.

We currently have a means of determining whether someone is telling the truth. It is not guaranteed 100% accurate, but with further technical investigation it probably could be. I am referring to the polygraph testing device that is generally rated just short of 100% accurate. Just the announcement that the government is expanding the use of polygraph testing in the activities mentioned above would act as a truth serum to everyone. Putting the polygraph into expanded operational use could return the control of our government back to the citizens like a real democracy.

The Composition of Our Government

Socialism provides benefits to the working class. Capitalism provides benefits to the wealthy investment class. Democracy provides "rule by the ruled" when it is not overwhelmed by big corporation money. The exploitation of the working class through replacement of American workers with foreign workers, lack of regulation of businesses, financial dependency on Wall Street, etc. verifies that the United States is primarily a capitalistic state. Enough jobs to give prosperity to the working class will not be available until control of our government is taken away from the big corporation money and given back to the people. The working class has the votes to do this, but most of them are influenced by political propaganda, political parties and big corporation money, which prevents this from happening. Wouldn't it be nice if all members of the working class would refuse to vote until Congress passes a bill on complete campaign finance reform where all campaign financing is paid by the government? Our votes aren't worth much anyway compared to five million dollars given each year to most members of Congress by big business. Even the preamble to the Constitution, "promote the general welfare," has been negated by big corporation money.

Our Health Care Dilemma

The tragic problem with health care in the United States is that the citizens are provided with health care <u>insurance</u> rather than the affordable health care that they need. Our current health care system is rated about thirty-nine in value as compared to the government controlled systems in the rest of the industrialized countries. President Obama promised us a single payer system in his campaign speeches. After he got into office he found out that such a "change" would cost him the financial support of about all of the big corporations that also control Congress. The best thing about his proposed health care plan was the public option to a government controlled system, but he dropped that "hot potato" as soon as he could. Providing health care for thirty million

Americans, people with pre-existing conditions, people that become critically ill, etc. sounds like a good idea, but the HMOs are free to raise prices whenever they desire, so unfortunately the other HMO members will have to foot the bill. His proposal is a boon to the HMO's and will probably to lead to from currently doubling our health care costs to tripling our costs in less than ten years. In order to pass a government controlled health care system in Congress we would first have to take the control of our government away from the big corporation money.

The Devastating Effects of Inflation

Inflation is very destructive to the standard of living of the working class and particularly to senior citizens. Politicians and news commentators rarely discuss inflation these days as if it is under control but my observations tell me that it is running out of control. The money I earned for my retirement years ago now has the purchasing power of less than ten percent of what it was worth when I earned it.

A large group of our citizens make their money by simply raising prices and forcing inflation. One example is the occupation of trading in futures. This activity was originally designed to allow businesses to hedge against future prices of materials required for their manufactured products. It was later modified to permit individuals and large hedge funds to bid on products and not ever take delivery but create a profit as if they had a virtual government printing press. Banks also create inflation by loaning more money than they have on deposit at a leverage value of ten to twenty times. Another example is the constant price increases in oil and gasoline prices. Committees in both houses of Congress concluded that these increases were caused primarily by trading of futures and not demand. If the Congress were functioning properly it would pass legislation to curtail inflation.

Ignoring the Real Solutions
to Our Economic Problems

If the citizens of the U.S. would use their own power of reasoning rather than accept the ideas of the paid politicians and the news media they would realize that big corporation money has purchased the prevention of any serious comments regarding the cause and solution to our current economic disaster. Discussions about our economic crisis do not contain any reference to outsourcing jobs to foreign countries, participation in the World Trade Organization where we cannot compete with $2/hr. labor and create huge trade deficits, visa programs where foreign workers replace American workers at a much lower cost, unfair trade agreements like NAFTA and China's 25% tariff on U.S. cars sold in China, and the U.S. Supreme Court identifying bribes as free speech so the system of controlling our government by big corporations can be strengthened.

It has finally gotten to the point where big corporation money can control how the average citizen thinks. Most citizens belong to political parties that take their votes and their money and give them nothing in return other than the joy of possibly beating the other party.

Creating Money Without
Creating Any Value

One of the main reasons why our economy will not restore prosperity to the working class is that the economic system has finally reached the threshold where the number of unproductive occupations in the U.S. has reached a harmful level. I am referring to those unproductive occupations where money is created without providing any goods or helpful services. One good example of this is the job of trading commodity futures where individuals, groups and hedging funds bid on products for which they have no intention of taking delivery, but extract huge profits by raising the prices. These operations are pure speculation and money manipulation that is devastating the working class by weakening the dollar and creating inflation, and which can also be identified as gambling, usually with someone else's money. Another example of unnecessary middleman type of occupations are the financial institutions including banks and Wall Street who reduce their funds available for loans to businesses and invest most of their funds betting on speculative transactions like derivatives.

Both the White House and Congress are aware of this problem but will do nothing to correct it as long as big business investors pay them not to take any action.

Save the Middle Class Economy

The way our economic system currently works the politicians and political analysts receive money from the big corporations and in return aid them in exploiting the middle class workers. The American workers are replaced with cheaper foreign workers through outsourcing, foreign worker visa programs, competition from $2/hr. foreign workers via the World Trade Organization, illegal immigration and unfair trade agreements like NAFTA and the 25% tariff on U.S. cars sold in China. There is little or no regulation of big business in the U.S., which results in excessive gas prices caused by commodity futures traders, a collapse of the housing market, banks using their funds for speculation rather than new business investments and increasing their leverage from ten percent to thirty percent and Wall Street extracting huge profits from our economy without giving anything to the public in return, except inflation.

Big corporation money has also used the politicians and particularly television to convince the public that the cause of our economic problems is the fault of big government. This is really ironic since big business controls our government and big business is the cause of our failed government with their struggle for increased profits.

There is no resolution to this problem with our economy until the public can think for themselves and realize that their enemy is big business, not big government. Then, maybe we can demand complete campaign finance reform and bring prosperity back to the working class by manufacturing and selling products right here within the U.S.

The Political System of the U.S.

Our political system has evolved not based on promoting the General welfare per our Constitution but based on cashing in on the vulnerability of the working class citizens concerning money. The main incentive of our system of politics has been the profits available to big business and the politicians. Big business contributes money and favors to politicians so they are permitted to exploit the working class. The politicians accept contributions from both big corporations and the citizens and still manage to convince many voters that the politicians are serving their interests. Part of this deceit is made possible by the distracting battle between the parties.

Neither Democrats nor the Republicans seek prosperity for the working class by stopping the replacement of American workers with cheaper foreign workers, stricter regulation of financial and commercial businesses, ceasing the practice of trading with $2/hr. countries, etc. The solution to all of this failing government is for Congress to pass complete campaign finance reform, but the big corporations pay them not to do it.

A large portion of this country's economy is being wasted on the scam of destructive politics, since politicians contribute nothing in the way of a product or helpful service to justify their existence.

Our New System of Government

The system of government in the United States has changed drastically in the recent years. We used to have a form of government resembling a democracy which was to a great extent "ruled by the ruled." Today we have a plutocracy, which is "ruled by the wealthy." Big business money controls our economy and determines the standard of living of the working class. `As a result, the rich are getting richer and the middle class and the poor are getting poorer.

In order to increase the profits of big business the working class is relegated to replacement of America labor with cheaper foreign labor, weak regulation of financial and commercial businesses to permit exploitation of the working class, trading with $2 per hour countries, etc. Our workers are struggling with lower wages and loss of jobs, but still big business money invested in political contributions and TV propaganda programs has convinced many of them that big government, their only hope for survival, is the culprit, and big business and politicians are their friends.

To get Congress to implement complete campaign finance reform and regain our democracy would require paying most of the members of Congress five million dollars each year, which is about what they are getting now from big business.

Failure of the Two-Party System

This two party contest diverts our attention from our economic crisis. Whichever party gets into power we will not get a solution to this problem because both parties are controlled by big corporation money. They also pay Congress and the White House to sanction outsourcing jobs to other countries, weakening regulation of businesses, trading with $2/hr. countries, entering into unfair trade agreements like NAFTA, etc. Yes, there is a difference between the two parties, but not concerning these major economic issues. The Republicans advertise tax breaks for the wealthy, reduction of social entitlements and complete elimination of regulation of businesses. The best your vote will do for you is to select the lesser of two evils because politicians are in the business of making money, not "promoting the general welfare." This Administration and any future administrations will not bring prosperity to the working class until the money is taken out of politics.

The only thing that I can see that the working class vote can obtain toward economic recovery is if we don't vote at all until Congress passes complete campaign finance reform where office holders cannot accept money from anyone and the government pays for all campaign expenses.

The Price of Political Parties

The cost to citizens for the operation of political parties is huge and all that the working class gets is gridlock on all economic and campaign affected issues and the promotion of corporate welfare, instead of the general welfare as required by our Constitution. One good example is the failure to change the existing law that anyone born in this country automatically is awarded citizenship. We cannot afford to give benefits to visitors to the United States. All members of Congress realize that this law established by the Constitution has now become destructive and should be discontinued, but party politics prevents any cooperative action on this problem. If one party tries to accomplish this, the other party must oppose it to prevent any successful legislation "by the enemy." The party that attempts this change will lose the Latino vote as well as the financial support of big corporations that thrive on cheap labor that visits the U.S. legally or illegally. If the members of Congress voted independently and were not bound to a political party or corporate money an amendment to the Constitution could easily be achieved. The existence of political parties in this country is detrimental to the working class and serves only the desires of the politicians, the political parties and the big corporations that finance them.

The Working Class Dilemma

The Working Class in the United States are becoming less prosperous while the wealthy investors are becoming more prosperous. The indicator of financial well- being called "the economy" has recently split into two separate sections, "the working class economy" and the "big corporation economy." When the big corporations replace American workers with cheaper foreign workers the big corporation economy prospers, while the working class economy suffers a financial loss. The better paying manufacturing and administrative jobs are being transferred to foreign workers by outsourcing, trading with $2/hr. labor countries like China, foreign worker visa programs, unfair trade agreements like NAFTA and illegal immigration.

The politicians have decided that the recession is over even though we have lost millions of jobs and entire industries to other countries. These losses of jobs are permanent so part of the working class will have to settle for low paying or temporary jobs in the service industry. The cure for all of this is complete campaign finance reform, but the big corporations pay member of Congress not to propose this change. Who is the enemy of the working class - big government as touted by the news media or big corporations that exploit the working class?

Evaluation of the Tea Party

The Tea Party is composed of groups of people around the United States that have gotten together to complain about the failure of the government to promote the general welfare as stated in the

Constitution. This movement has been aided and influenced by Republican Party politicians.

Tea Party members' desires are determined mainly by what they hear from politicians on TV and elsewhere and has been formulated and promoted by the big corporation money. This strong wave of political propaganda establishes the Tea Party agenda, getting them to overlook the real needs of the working class that actually dictates their standard of living. This propaganda program convinces them that government regulation of business, the only means available to stop exploitation of the working class, is bad. As a result big corporations can continue replacing American workers with cheaper foreign workers. Also, socialism is bad, so we should reduce benefits to the working class, like Social Security and Medicare. They are right about big government being bad, but only when controlled by big corporation money as exists today.

The Tea Party members have ignored the greatest government injustice of all that concerns the origination of their name - "taxation without representation". Yes, they do get to vote for the members of Congress, but the members end up representing the big corporation money in all economic legislation.

Enemies of the Working Class

If you want to win a war you have to be able to identify your enemy. This is also true in the struggle for political control of the United States, which defines the living conditions of its citizens. Big corporations seek maximum profits so they devise ways to replace American workers with cheaper foreign labor and reduce corporate taxes. This is accomplished by giving large contributions and favors to government office holders and to both political parties, usually through lobbyists.

In their speeches politicians speak favorably about promoting the general welfare as our Constitution dictates, but in their actions they promote corporate welfare as they are paid to do by the big corporations. Most politicians, and particularly members of Congress, are seeking their own personal gains and are not doing what is best for the average American citizen. The politicians will not provide our government with needed complete campaign finance reform where all campaigns are paid for by the government, and office holders cannot accept political contributions or favors from anyone. Members of the working class should be aware of the fact that most big corporations and politicians and both political parties are the enemies of the working class. They are all making money by exploiting the working class.

Reverse the Control of Our Government

It is requested that the United States Supreme Court take the control of our government away from big business investors and give it back to the working class citizens.

Under our current system of government big business investors hire and fund lobbyists (40,000 in Washington D.C.) who negotiate the details and price of profit favorable legislation with members of Congress and the Whitehouse. This is verified by the fact that the following major needs of the working class cannot even brought up for a vote in Congress:

1. Stop the practice of replacing American labor with cheaper foreign labor. This includes outsourcing jobs to foreign countries, work program visas and illegal immigration.

2. Correct all unfair trade agreements and enforce rules regarding child labor, slave labor and working conditions.

3. Withdraw from the WTO and concentrate on the manufacture and sale of all products within the United States where possible. Eliminate our huge trade deficit by realizing that over $20/hr. American labor cannot compete with less than $2/hr. foreign labor.

4. Replace our current maximizing failed health care insurance system with a proven universal single payer system with half the cost and improved service as in all of the other industrialized countries.

5. Strictly regulate all big businesses and particularly financial institutions so they cannot

exploit the working class as is the current practice.

6.   Bring back our troops from Iraq, Afghanistan and all other foreign countries that are held there by lucrative no-bid contracts. (And the list goes on.)

The United States Supreme Court should direct the Congress to initiate complete campaign financing reform where only taxpayer dollars are used and no office holder shall accept political donations of money or favors from anyone. The basis for changing the current control of government could be the lack of representation of the voters in favor of big business money and preferred access to office holders by lobbyists, which is denied to citizens without contributions, plus returning to a democratic form of government (rule by the ruled) rather that our present capitalistic (rule by money) form of government, plus returning to promoting the general welfare (not corporate welfare) as per our Constitution.

Restore the Value of Voting

When citizens vote in our current government elections they assume they are promoting the principles promised by the candidate. This is a false assumption because most candidates end up promoting the principles that have been paid for by big business investors or are required by their political party. Both political parties give big business what they need to maximize profits, so we see no bills passed in Congress to stop the replacement of American labor with cheap foreign labor, expand regulation of both commercial and financial businesses, discontinue trading with countries with $2/hr. labor, bring our troops home from all foreign countries, correct all unfair trade agreements, etc. The Republican Party goes a step further and attempts to reduce entitlements for the working class and decrease taxes for businesses. Our economical deficit should be reduced by diminishing the greed of big business investors, not by making the poor poorer.

Voting has become less meaningful for the working class because they are not properly represented by the candidates when they get into office. In fact, the working class would be better off not voting at all until Congress passes complete campaign finance reform where the government pays for all campaigns and office holders cannot accept money or favors from anyone.

Permanent Job Losses

Pundits and politicians discussing the poor economy always end up stating that our job recovery is going to be very slow. They know why, but will not tell you why, because big corporations pay them, or their TV channels, not to disclose the real reason for the inability of job recovery in the U.S.

The approach for increasing profits for this past decade has been to replace American workers with cheaper foreign workers. This results in permanent job losses for individuals and often entire industries like manufacturing TVs, clothing, steel, etc. and they are working on the car industry. If the news media cannot discuss the reasons for our permanent job losses they also cannot offer any solutions, but I can. Outsourcing our jobs to foreign countries and foreign worker visa programs must be stopped and reversed. We cannot continue trading with countries like China that have $2/hr. labor resulting in huge trade deficits. The U.S. must implement a program of manufacturing and selling most all products right here in the United States. To accomplish this we must take the money out of campaigns and politics and have the government finance all campaigns. This is the only way Congress can pass bills that will benefit the working class and stop providing big corporations with cheap labor and large tax cuts as is currently being done.

Some of our best high paying labor jobs have been shipped overseas, leaving the unemployed in no position to compete with cheaper illegal immigrants for the remaining low paying service jobs.

Political Parties in the U.S.

The two major political parties in the U.S. have been established so that small groups of politicians can influence large groups of citizens and make money by soliciting contributions from the citizens as well as big business investors who are willing to pay for the lucrative support of the citizens' representatives. The first step of this setup is to convince the citizens that this particular political party is looking out for the financial interests and well-being of the citizens, even if their true actions are to make more money for the politicians that control the party. This is verified by the fact that politicians aid big corporations in exploiting the working class with such programs as replacing American workers with cheaper foreign workers and reducing corporation taxes. One of the most effective devices of the political parties is to divide the interests of the citizens so they end up fighting each other's party rather than fighting big business investors who are exploiting the working class. More and more we see situations where one party will refuse to agree to a benefit for the working class in order to prevent the other party from passing a successful bill. Political parties are a nonproductive business and they offer nothing of value like products or services, and making money takes president over representing the citizens.

Citizens should not be locked into political parties but should vote and act independently based on what is best for themselves personally, but give priority to what is best for the average citizen.

A Misinformed Middle Class

The standard of living of the middle class has been going down for the past ten years with no prospect of ever regaining prosperity. The reason for this is that big business investors that control the Congress and the White House through contributions and favors are free to replace American workers with cheaper foreign workers, avoid regulation of financial and commercial businesses, trade with $2/hr. countries, and the list goes on. Many middle class citizens are satisfied with this exploitation because they are living well, but most of them are suffering financially, some being convinced that government help is destructive.

It is unfortunate that big business investors have been able to convince many of the middle class citizens that they should oppose any actions by the government to help them because according to most politicians and news commentators "big government is bad." In reality, government is the only means of stopping big business investors from exploiting the middle class. One of our big problems is that the middle class is misinformed concerning who is hurting them, it's big business, not big government.

Citizens should figure it out by themselves and not be influenced by money- making politicians.

Promoting the General Welfare?

All of the citizens should be aware of the fact that on most major economic issues there will be no "promoting the general welfare" as stated in our Constitution. Money from big business investors does not permit actions that raise the standard of living for the working class in the U.S., and the U.S. Supreme Court insures the continuing control of Congress and the White House by big corporations when they sanctioned contributions by big business to politicians. This problem has been verified by the Health Care Reform Bill that has retained our current HMO health care insurance system that doubles the cost of health care in the U.S. and provides a service that is rated 37th. in the world. The next major bill offered by this Congress concerns financial reform, which has been equally watered down to not include the strict regulations needed and the reduction of the size of the financial institutions that are currently too big to fail.

There will be no action to regain prosperity for the working class until complete campaign finance reform is installed to take the control of our government from the big business investors and give it back to the people to restore our side-tracked democracy. Another factor that makes it difficult to pass any major legislation is the sixty votes required in the Senate that the political parties use to defeat each other.

Where Is the Change?

There was supposed to be a major change in the operation of our government but it just didn't happen. As a Democrat of long standing I am disappointed that most major government functions are going about the same as under the Bush Administration. President Obama now states that our troops won't be out of Iraq in sixteen months, but some will still be there for several years. Any health care reform will still include the HMO's that have been jacking up the costs sky high. A single payer system, which is the way to drastically reduce costs, is not under consideration. Hundreds of billions of dollars are still being given to the greedy lending institutions that cannot be trusted. Big business is still free to exchange American workers for cheaper foreign workers. There is no talk about a complete campaign financing system paid for only by taxpayer funds so the control of our government by big business can be stopped. We are still attempting to compete in a global trading system even though our labor costs are ten times greater than many of the other countries The corruption of government office holders is still at an unacceptable level.

Positions change, but it seems that all politicians operate about the same on major issues and just follow the dollar.

Big Government vs. Big Business

There has always been a lot of politicians and their followers that have talked about the negative attributes of a big government. This idea has been initiated by the Republicans and repeated by many Democrats who want to justify campaign contributions received and claim to save the citizens from the abuses of big government such as high taxes, regulation, wasteful spending, expensive entitlements and progressive taxation. Some say that government can't do anything right, but we rarely are told when big business makes mistakes because the consumer quietly pays the bill.

Big government itself is not bad, but any size of government that is controlled by the greed of big business money is very bad for the average citizen. When big business dictates through over 40,000 lobbyists how the U.S. should replace our workers with cheap foreign labor in order to increase their profits and all regulation should be set aside, it is time for the public to recognize that big business is the enemy of the American working class. If you can't identify the enemy, you will never win the battle. One of the most important functions of a good government is to protect its working citizens from being exploited by the greed of big business, and the lack of this protection is the cause of our current economic disaster.

Save Our Automobile Industry

The importers of automobiles and automobile parts that control our Congress continue to force our car manufacturers to compete with foreign countries whose labor costs are about one-tenth of our labor costs. It looks like we are about to lose another industry to foreign competition.

Because we don't actually have a democracy (ruled by the ruled) the solution to this problem is not available. The solution is, of course, to restrict the sale of cars in this country to completely U.S. built cars and parts, as China has been doing with its 25% tariff on U.S. cars sold in China, resulting in a huge trade surplus for them since they also have low labor costs.

To prevent us from correcting this problem the conservative politicians have created another "dirty word" called "protectionism." They have convinced the American people that to protect our workers from cheap foreign labor is bad for the country. And it works! The importers are making lots of money and American workers are sacrificing their good-paying manufacturing jobs. When we finally go to war with China we won't even have a viable manufacturing base.

Socialism vs. Capitalism

Conservative politicians have created a new "dirty word." Whenever they dislike a proposal giving a government controlled benefit to the working class they label it as socialism, implying that socialism is something bad. The truth of the matter is that socialism is bad for big business profits, but good for the working class recipients of the benefit. One of the things they dislike the most is socialized medicine, even though it has given affordable universal medical care to all of the other industrialized countries of the world for half of our costs. The United States claims to be a democratic state, but we are not actually "ruled by the ruled" but instead are " ruled by big business money." The White House and 535 members of Congress will tell you that if they are truthful. We are currently in a capitalistic state, where big money makes all of the political decisions, so you don't get such things as affordable government controlled health care, outlawing replacing American labor with cheaper foreign labor, stopping unfair foreign trade, stopping illegal immigration, and the list goes on. Capitalism is good for big business investors. Socialism is good for the working class who need to be protected from exploitation by big corporations.

Middleman Businesses that
Only Exploit Consumers

There are many businesses in this country that do not justify their existence. Businesses that take on the function of a middleman and operate between the producer or service and the consumers and contribute only an administrative or price setting function are unnecessary middlemen.

HMO's are an example of a middleman business that performs administrative functions for health care services at double the normal costs. Future speculative trading of oil and commodities are examples of middleman businesses that offer no business function other than increasing the price of a product to extract large unearned profits. A new middleman service is now being advertised on TV offering to pay your car repair bills. The uninformed consumer must pay the administrative costs, profits and the repair bill for this service and end up over -paying. Only catastrophic losses that cannot be paid by the individual should be covered by insurance.

The Whitehouse and the Congress should eliminate these middleman businesses, but they will not because both of them receive large contributions from these businesses.

Health Care Insurance vs. Health Care

It has been proven that private insurance companies have doubled the cost of health care in the United States as compared to costs in the other industrialized countries. In their attempt to maximize profits, HMOs have also denied service to many high- risk patients resulting in financial disaster and deaths. Even though our government has successfully provided Medicare, Medicaid and veteran's health care programs for years, paid political pundits say that they are not to be trusted. They want you, instead, to trust the greedy insurance companies that have devastated the working class with a lack of reliable and affordable health care coverage.

The health care bill being considered in Congress is nothing but an invitation for the HMOs to continue the current failed system, with a bonus of thirty million more assigned members and the taxpayers paying for the added participants and the added high- risk coverage, and this statement comes from a Democrat. Both the Congressional Budget Office and the General Accounting Office have concluded that the cost savings of a single payer system would pay for an affordable universal health care system.

The Politics of Our Government

This is an analysis of why the U.S. Government is not providing its citizens with the kinds of programs that the average American needs and why this country is in our current economic and financial crisis.

The politicians that determine the living conditions of our citizens are operating in a very corrupt system. In order to get elected into office and stay there they must retain the financial backing of the big corporations who, in turn, require cooperation on issues that affect their profits. Citizens have limited representation in Congress on many vital issues like the following: No low cost government controlled health care as enjoyed in Europe and Canada. Both Republicans and Democrats offer the citizens health care

Insurance, not a true health care program. Prescription drugs are sold for half of our price in other countries. Millions of living wage jobs are given to cheaper foreign foreign laborers. There are many other issues like illegal immigration, foreign worker visas, unfair trade agreements, lack of business regulation and forty thousand lobbyists.

Less than one hundred members of Congress have signed a petition to install taxpayer financing of all political campaigns but most politicians prefer their current financial gains.

The Rich Get Richer

The Bush administration is in the process of proposing a 700 million dollar bailout for financial corporations that created a major financial disaster in the U.S. through their greediness of questionable loans. This occurred within many loan companies because all regulations were completely removed. Instead of holding the loan companies responsible for the losses of their bad loans this administration shifts the burden to the taxpayers, many of which are also losing their homes. The reason for this unusual action is that the Bush administration is indebted to the big business investors for their contributions of money and favors, but are not indebted to the taxpayers. They claim that this action is necessary immediately to save the country's financial structure. The excuse that it will cost us more if we don't bail them out is unproven and typical of this administration's scare tactics.

These loan companies are guilty of deceitful business practices and should go out of business so they don't do this again and as a warning for future businesses. Our government should help the victims who lost their homes, not the perpetrators. One thing I know for sure is that this is another act by the Bush administration to make the rich richer and the poor poorer.

__Manufacturing Economy__
__vs. Financial Economy__

After WWII the United States concentrated its efforts on an economy primarily engaged in manufacturing products that were to be sold mostly within the United States. Both the Clinton and Bush administrations changed to a course of a financial economy by promoting cheaper foreign labor and financial manipulation and deregulation of the loaning and trading markets. Many programs have been employed that are devastating the middle class and the poor to increase profits for the big business investors. Global trading has been expanded to the point where it becomes obvious that $20/hr. American workers cannot compete with $2/hr. foreign workers. American workers are also being replaced by cheaper foreign workers through visa programs, outsourcing jobs and illegal immigration. Meanwhile, financial trading has been completely unregulated resulting in huge profits for financial traders and loaning agencies at a severe cost to the consumers. Trading in futures serves only one purpose and that is to raise the price of commodities by speculators who never take delivery on anything. Credit card companies are free to do as they please. Loaning institutions are allowed to issue loans for ten to thirty times their liquid capital. Our politicians were given large campaign contributions and other favors to allow all of this to happen. We need to return to a manufacturing economy in order to regain prosperity for the working class.

Only One Health Care Solution

Both the Congressional Budget Office and the General Accounting Office have concluded that a proven single payer health care system would provide affordable health care for all Americans without any additional costs. Numerous studies performed by unbiased groups have concluded that a single payer system will give us better medical service than our present insurance system.

If the Whitehouse and the Congress could just give up their big business contributions and favors we could get affordable universal health care plus save 45,000 lives each year for those that currently cannot afford to purchase insurance.

Our current HMO health care insurance system has devastated U.S. health care for the working class, but it would be a mistake to allow the same insurance companies to control an expansion of the same system as proposed by Congress.

No Solution to Our Economic Crisis?

With all of the intelligent people in this country it is inconceivable that no one has offered a viable solution to our economic crisis. A stimulus plan provides only temporary relief and does not create permanent jobs. After much consideration I have come to the conclusion that many people are aware of a solution but the financial gains to be obtained by not solving the problem are more desirable than the act of giving relief to the middle class and the poor who are suffering. One possible solution is to return to the system of manufacturing and selling products within the U.S. Another is to restore regulations to the loaning institutions.

To prove the point that no solution is forthcoming, look at what the politicians in control are doing now. They have given huge sums of money to Wall Street and big banks that are run by the very people who exacerbated the economic crisis through unregulated transactions. There is no planning or accountability regarding the bailout and thus far, no indication of any progress. The greed of exploiting the average citizen by big corporations goes on and on because that is what is desired by the people that control our government. Are there any politicians left who will "promote the general welfare" as our Constitution requires?

Politicians Exploit the Workers

Many of our politicians have no problem with giving billions to Wall Street without any strings attached, but are against saving the jobs of the failing auto industry, and they place the blame on the labor unions. The auto industry is failing because of unfair global competition and the financial burden of giving a living wage, health care and pensions to the workers. Wall Street failed because of greed for profit on unregulated loans.

Both the Republicans and the Democrats give tax benefits and other favors to big corporations to obtain campaign contributions, but the Republicans go one step further and reduce benefits to the workers. The solution is complete campaign finance reform where the taxpayers provide all of the money for political campaigns and a revision of our economy so American labor does not have to compete with foreign labor, which is one-tenth of the cost of our labor. We used to manufacture and sell products right within the U.S. and it created prosperity. Stimulating the economy with trillions of taxpayer dollars is

a temporary, not the permanent fix we need to get those millions of manufacturing jobs back from foreign countries.

.

Where Are the Jobs?

It is amazing how the politicians can get on TV and state that the country has to create more jobs and they completely ignore the real reasons for the job loss and offer no viable solution to the problem. The explanation for this situation is that they are well aware of the causes of the job loss and the solution to the problem but are paid by big business investors with contributions and favors not to take the proper corrective action.

The cause of job losses is that American labor has been replaced by cheaper foreign labor so big business can make higher profits. Job visa programs and illegal immigration permit foreign workers to fill American jobs. Trading with foreign countries in the WTO gives $2/hr. foreign labor a huge advantage over $20/hr. American labor as indicated by our large trade deficits. Trade agreements favor foreign countries and U.S. importers.

The solution to the problem is to start manufacturing and selling most all products within the United States and eliminate all job visa programs and illegal immigration. The politicians never discuss this on TV or debate it in Congress.

Disappointed With the
U.S. Supreme Court

Members of the U.S. Supreme Court are appointed for life so they don't have to be concerned about losing their jobs if someone doesn't like their decisions. But there still is the remaining problem about allegiance to the political party that put them in office. A good example is the Presidential Election of 2000 where they stopped the recount in Palm Beach County based on "equal protection" but were not equal at all when they failed to provide a recount in all counties, and thus completely stopped a recount that was fully justified.

An even better example of the U.S. Supreme Court failing to do their job is the lack of action regarding our corrupt legislative system where big business investors give money and favors to members of Congress through forty thousand lobbyists leaving the citizens not represented on issues that concern business profits. This is why we cannot have a low cost government controlled health care system or jobs that have been given to cheap foreign workers. Like everyone else that holds a government office, the members of the U.S. Supreme Court are acting like politicians. Though the ruined credit market is of primary importance at this time, we must resolve the loss of jobs before obtaining any real financial relief for the working class in this country.

Double Pronged Bad Economy

There are three major reasons for the loss of jobs. The first is the practice of outsourcing jobs and the manufacturing function to foreign countries to take advantage of cheap labor. The second is the negotiation of unfair free trade agreements like the one that blocks the sale of cars in China with a 25 % tariff. The third is global trading where our over $20/hr. manufacturing labor cannot compete with the less than $2/hr. labor in some other countries so we end up with a huge trade deficit and a loss of millions of jobs. All three of these reasons for the loss of jobs are the result of our big business investors pursuing a program of replacing American labor with cheap foreign labor. Congress goes along with this program because they want to continue receiving large campaign contributions and other favors from big business. The U.S. Supreme Court could stop it by requiring taxpayer financed campaigns based on the lack of representation of taxpayers.

The Cause of Our Economic Crisis

Our economy and our government are probably in the worst condition that they have ever been. This was caused by the greed of business corporations and individuals. The practice of taking whatever they can and disregarding what problems it creates for other individuals has always been present but never to the extent that it currently prevails.

Taking jobs away from hard-working American citizens and giving them to cheaper foreign workers is not only acceptable but it is also condoned and promoted by the current administration. This is done by every means that is possible including the increasing of foreign imports, the relocation of manufacturing facilities to foreign countries, visa programs to bring in foreign workers, outsourcing of U.S. jobs to foreign countries like India and fostering illegal immigration. There is a lot of profit involved in switching to cheaper foreign labor but it denies American workers a job with a fair living wage.

Reducing the federal interest rates or giving money to Wall Street will not correct the situation. The only permanent solution is to provide more jobs to the citizens of this country. Unfortunately, politicians cannot make money by bringing our jobs back to the United Stated, so there is no Incentive to do this.

U.S. Government Failure

The United States Government is not functioning properly as indicated by the following failures that are purposely created: 1. There is no low cost universal health care program like those available in most other wealthy industrialized countries. 2. We should not be involved in the current global trading program because our labor costs are too high to be competitive and we end up with a huge loss of jobs and trading deficits. This includes our program of "free trade", which is not "fair trade". 3. We do not regulate businesses and this has resulted in a severe home mortgage and loan crisis. 4. Current government policies have caused an increase in inequality between the wealthy investors and executives compared to the working class and a general downgrading of the middle class and the poor. 5. Millions of better-paying manufacturing and other jobs have been outsourced to foreign labor.

There is a common cause for all of these problems. It is the large campaign contributions given by big business to legislators, which are needed to retain their jobs. The United States

Supreme Court could resolve the situation by requiring complete taxpayer only campaign finance reform based on the lack of taxpayer representation by the legislators and the inequality of lobbyists' access to government officials.

Another Round of Gas
Price Manipulation

Last year oil future speculators hit the top on oil and gas price manipulation so they had to drop way down to start generating big profits again. If they take turns raising oil prices all of them make huge profits. One future trader made three billion dollars in a single year. It's the consumers that pay for this.

Both the House and the Senate had committee meetings on the excessive gas prices and both concluded that they were caused primarily by trading speculators. Nothing was done to correct this important problem because big business contributors want no part of regulation.

Future trading speculators never take delivery of the product so they perform no service like manufacturing or distribution. Their only function is to raise the price and make a profit. Fleecing the public is an acceptable practice even though it does not promote the general welfare as our Constitution states.

Analysis of Our Economy Crisis

In order to resolve our economic crisis we must fully analyze how we got into our current dilemma and use the information to construct a solution to return to where we were during the prosperity we enjoyed after WWII. Most politicians have already done this but reject the proper conclusion for personal financial reasons.

The cause of the crisis is that big corporations gave money and favors to our members of Congress and, in return, were permitted to replace American labor with cheap foreign labor and to offer unsafe loans. Government gave billions of dollars to allow these greedy financial institutions to survive but did not resolve the working class jobs problem. Congress is working on new loan regulations, but it isn't easy to oppose the money offered by the big financial corporations. A solution to the loss of our millions of good-paying permanent jobs has not been initiated and all that this administration is offering is a temporary fix in the form of a stimulus package.

There appears to be only one permanent solution to our economic crisis and that is to manufacture and sell products within the United States. We need more living-wage jobs for the unemployed and low- wage workers so they can support themselves and our government. The purpose of our government should be to provide living wage jobs to our workers, not greater profits to big businesses.

Correcting a Failed Government

It has been pretty well proven that big business investors have taken over the control of our government through contributions to politicians. This needs to be corrected.

Congress could pass a complete campaign finance reform bill that would direct the government to finance all political campaigns and prevent anyone from giving money or favors to potentially or elected office holders, but they are paid by big business not to take this action. The U.S. Supreme Court could force Congress to invoke complete campaign finance reform, but most of its members have an obligation to the party that gave them the job and are willing to interpret the Constitution to favor the power of money. They chose to deny the citizens representation, permit lobbying by only the wealthy and fail to " promote the general welfare."

It seems almost impossible to break big business's control over our government and return the working class to prosperity. Short of a revolution, the only solution I can think of is for the citizens to stop voting until the politicians give us complete campaign finance reform and the programs that big business has blocked, like single payer health care.

The Economy Issue

The financial status of the average worker has gotten very depressing with the lack of good paying jobs, high prices for gasoline, health care and other needs and skyrocketing deficits. Many believe that the main reason for the closing of manufacturing plants and the shipping of jobs overseas is that our over $20/hour labor costs cannot compete with the less that $2/hour cheap foreign labor. Big business has experienced huge profits under this global trading, and members of Congress go along with it because of the large campaign contributions, other favors and the prospect of a lifetime in office.

Global trading brings with it loss of jobs and wages, a huge trade deficit, defective and unsafe products and a government that has to borrow money from China to avoid bankruptcy. Instead of consumers getting lower prices, they are actually higher because only foreign countries and import distributors gain the benefits of cheap foreign labor since goods are always sold at the highest price possible.

The solution to this globalization tragedy is to manufacture and sell most of our products in the U.S. like we did over a decade ago. This sounds like protectionism, which our business oriented politicians have labeled as a dirty word.

Purpose of Government :

Investors vs. Workers

What should be the primary goal of the U.S. Government, to provide financial gains for investors or to provide living wage jobs for the citizens of this country? The Constitution says we should promote the general welfare, and does not mention the corporate welfare. Most religions will go along with this idea and so will most of the citizens of this country. So what is the problem? The problem is that corporations are not human, and thus not humane. They only look at the bottom line on their profit and loss statements. In order to obtain the greatest profit in this global economy they will chose cheap foreign labor in preference to a living wage for American workers. We need investors that will establish businesses to create good jobs for Americans but should not permit the establishment of businesses that hire cheap foreign labor. The real benefactors of cheap foreign labor are the foreign countries and the distributors of their products in the U.S. American citizens lose their good-paying jobs and are thus supporting the citizens of these foreign countries. Prices eventually end up in accordance with the old economic rule - whatever the traffic will bear, so there no price reductions when cheaper labor is used.

There are a lot of people in this country making out fine with this new cheap foreign labor system, but the rich are getting richer and the poor are getting poorer, and our Constitution is getting ignored.

The Real Cause of High

Oil and Gas Prices

The recent Congressional debates on high gas prices exposes the practice of politicians clouding an issue in order to allow big business to continue exploiting the American public. They are trying to convince us that our high gas prices are a result of the normal economic law of supply and demand.

There currently is no shortage of oil. The demand for oil has actually decreased, but the price of oil has still increased. There are other factors that affect the price of oil and gas such as the value of the U.S. dollar, speculation future trading and unfair gas pricing practices. At this particular time the primary cause of our high oil and gas prices is due to speculation future trading. If we increase the supply of oil or replace it with another source of energy the speculators will still keep bidding up the price of energy because that is how they make their billions of dollars of profit off of the American public each year.

The only solution to the current high oil and gas prices is to stop the speculation future trading. Republican legislators are fighting against this solution and propose instead increasing our supply of oil by drilling along our coasts and in Alaska.

Increased drilling will eventually reduce our dependency on foreign oil, but it will have little effect on our current high gas price problem.

Lack of Government Regulation

Big business interests that control TV and other news media have long been promoting their program for eliminating the regulation of businesses. This has opened the way for big business to exploit the middle class and the poor in this country. Government regulation is absolutely essential to promote the general welfare as stated in the U.S. Constitution. It is obvious that this administration's hands-off policy toward regulation has resulted in large mortgage companies attempting to fleece citizens with adjustable excess interest rates that have now devastated our economy. They have also given financial grants to pharmaceutical companies for research, and the lack of regulation has allowed them to charge U.S. citizens twice as much for the resulting medicines as they charge foreign countries like Canada. The lack of needed regulation has permitted energy companies, such as gasoline refineries, to charge us whatever they want in order to receive huge profits. Government regulation is dearly needed to correct the current unfair free trading and the outsourcing of jobs to foreign countries. In the last few decades there has been a movement against big government. They want you to believe that big government is an enemy of its citizens. This is not true, as evidenced by such successful big government programs as Social Security and Medicare. We need an increase in the kind of government that helps its citizens increase their standard of living.

Misusing the Constitution

Public speakers and particularly politicians often use the U.S. Constitution to substantiate a point for which they have no reasonable proof. One of my favorite examples is a statement made by a member of the U.S. Supreme Court, which is often repeated by politicians. It concerns the right of lobbyists to give members of Congress large campaign contributions, which is guaranteed by the free speech amendment to the U.S.

Constitution. In reality, giving large amounts of money to legislators in exchange for something like cheap foreign labor or tax breaks is pure and simple corruption in our government, but it is being presented as a means of expressing one's desires, akin to free speech.

Like many other contested actions that often arise there is no statement that validates campaign contributions in the Constitution, so then it becomes a game of interpretation using any description present that may have a vague connection to what is desired. The founding fathers had no idea of all of the political problems that would arise in the future, not even the right of women to vote.

We should not conclude that the U.S. Constitution is the final word in all political conflicts. The final word should be what is currently considered best for the average citizen of this country.

Why Isn't Our Government Functioning?

The financial catastrophes and the low standard of living of the middle class and the poor in this country is the result of a government that is not functioning. Our huge financial deficit just keeps on growing with no solution in sight. The "free" trade policy has also created an out-of - control trading deficit because the agreed conditions are always unfair to the U.S. Global trading has been established, where our over $20 / hour labor cannot compete with the less that $2 / hour labor of many other countries. The unnecessary war in Iraq is killing and injuring our young people, creating a great financial burden and degrading our leadership in the world. Inflation is excessive and energy prices have been pushed up by speculation, price manipulation and the devalued dollar. Many of our best jobs have been transferred to other countries. Many of our laws, like illegal immigration and product country of origin labeling, have been ignored.

The solution to all of this is to take the control of our government away from the big business investors so we can regulate our business economy to favor the American workers rather than the big business investors. The start would be to have all election campaigns financed by the taxpayers.

The Functioning of Our Government

Things are not going well the way our government is functioning. It is supposed to represent a democracy that is "ruled by the ruled," but instead is a capitalistic state ruled by the power of money. Wealthy corporations give money and favors to our legislators and the White House and obtain in return huge tax reductions, free access to our natural resources plus the restraint of regulation so they can practice price gouging, exploitation of the public and control over health care, energy, pharmaceuticals, foreign trade and the use of cheap foreign labor.

Our political system has degenerated to the existence of 35,000 lobbyists in Washington D.C. who act as negotiators for large corporations that want to avoid the criminal responsibility for their purchase of tax relief and other favors.

There is an obvious solution to all of this malfunctioning of our government - complete campaign finance reform whereby the taxpayers pay for all political campaigns. Of course, any legislator that seriously attempts to accomplish this may experience a short term in office due to lack of funds.

Government Office Holders
Are Overly Generous

The existence of 35,000 lobbyists in Washington D.C. verifies that a lot of money and favors pass between government office holders and big business corporations. The corporation must receive much more than they give back to the office holders because their take in the exchange must be shared among the many executives and owners. Thus the office holder must be very generous with their tax reductions and favors and there are signs that they have been overly generous since many big businesses now pay little or no actual taxes. This means that the working class in this country has become the recipient of a huge tax burden that threatens their financial survival.

One of the largest favors given to big business is the promise of less regulation so the working class can be exploited to the fullest extent by sending their jobs overseas to take advantage of cheaper foreign labor and by price gouging consumer costs, especially in the areas of health care and energy.

This whole problem could be resolved by passing complete campaign finance reform whereby all costs are paid by the taxpayers using money saved by canceling all corporate welfare.

Health Insurance or Health Care?

Most Republicans say that our citizens need more health <u>insurance</u> while most Democrats say that they need more health <u>care</u>. Republicans, of course, would like to privatize most all of the needs of U.S. citizens and minimize the government's efforts to provide these needs. They privatized K.P. duty in the mess halls in Iraq and suffered the risk of terrorist killings. The attempt to privatize and degrade Social Security fell short of votes needed.

Health insurance brings business investors into the picture who can act as middle men as they purchase something in quantity but add no value to it and just sell it to the public to make a profit. This raises the price of health care drastically as we all have noticed over the last several years. A government run health care program would eliminate the profit and some of the administrative costs and thus make health care cheaper and available to everyone as currently done successfully in other countries.

It's true; a government controlled health care plan would represent a redistribution of the wealth from the rich to the poor. Many people believe this should not be a function of our government, but many more people believe it should, as does the Constitution of the U.S. in "promote the general welfare." Congress should not work on legislation to provide health insurance to more U.S. citizens but should work on legislation to provide health care at a much lower cost to everyone.

The Truth Could Benefit

The Working Class

The citizens of this country are being deceived on almost a daily basis and it is hurting them both financially and physically. Members of Congress are supposed to be representing the voters who put them in office, but are they are primarily representing the big corporations that give them large campaign contributions and other favors. Are all of the judges in our courts completely unbiased in handing down their decisions? Are politicians and the news media truthful in their comments concerning the real cause of our poor economy? Are Wall Street and other investment brokers being fair to the public when they manipulate investments? And the list goes on.

We currently have a means of determining whether someone is telling the truth. It is not guaranteed 100% accurate, but with further technical investigation it probably could be. I am referring to the polygraph testing device that is generally rated just short of 100% accurate. Just the announcement that the government is expanding the use of polygraph testing in the activities mentioned above would act as a truth serum to everyone. Putting the polygraph into expanded operational use could return the control of our government back to the citizens like a real democracy.

Distracting the Voters

Our political parties distract the voters from the important issues such as replacing American workers with foreign workers, unequal distribution of the wealth, corruption of office holders, etc. Television and the rest of the news media make their money by helping businesses and politicians exploit the working class, and they avoid attacking these important issues in order to increase their own profits. These issues are mentioned, but are rarely discussed in any serious detail that would influence the public. The fighting between the political parties is given a high priority, even though both parties support big business investors on all major economic issues as they are paid to do with campaign contributions and other favors. The political parties do disagree on some issues, such as the Republican goals of reducing social benefits to the working class (Social Security, etc.), large tax breaks for the wealthy and eliminating the regulation of businesses. The resulting devastation to the working class citizens could be resolved starting with taking the money out of politics by Congress passing complete campaign finance reform where all campaigns are financed only by taxpayer funds.

The Power of Television

Newspapers use to be the major influential form of news media and advertising, but today top honors go to the TV channels who have gained a strong influence over the American public. Audio visual advertising and political pundits can fleece the viewers much more easily than when using printed newspapers and magazines. Huge audiences can be accessed and sold belts with magnets that will reduce your weight, or air purifiers that have no fans or filters that will purify your air. Many commercials do not discuss the value of their product, but utilize conversation that is more entertaining to the public. Politicians can use the TV to get your votes and your financial contributions. More recently TV companies were permitted to own multiple channels to "prove" to you that what they promote is a fact. Fox News has created a large audience by telling the

Republicans what they want to hear, as paid for by big business investors. To say that our TV industry needs more regulation is putting it mildly. I would rather see the TV industry run by a fair government than by our current greedy big business investors. The power of television is in the wrong hands.

How Corrupt is Corrupt?

We have all heard statements that our government is corrupt, but according to our politicians it is not corrupt enough to ever be given any serious discussion. When your government has been changed from a democracy (ruled by the ruled) to a plutocracy (ruled by money) this represents the top level of corruption. Over half of our members of Congress have been purchased with large campaign contributions and other favors and the White House has received the highest campaign contributions in the history of our government. The working class pays for all of this indirectly, and they get outsourcing of jobs, little regulation of greedy businesses, no government health care system like other industrialized countries, large tax breaks for the wealthy big business investors, and the list goes on.

We need to take the money out of politics through complete campaign finance reform where all elections are paid for by the taxpayers, and then get rid of the political parties.

Leaders in Exploiting the Working Class

Both General Electric and Apple are leading the way for big businesses to exploit the working class by replacing American workers with cheaper foreign workers. They accomplish this goal by giving large campaign contributions and other favors to members of Congress and the White House with the help of many politicians, and they hire lobbyists to handle the messy details. To distract us from this devastating activity they run TV commercials showing how American workers are thriving and enjoying their jobs at an American company. Since most of the employees of both companies are Chinese working in their own countries, why don't they show mostly Chinese employees on TV working in China? This would be unfavorable public relations to show to the American working class citizens.

When our government loaned money to the dying auto industry that appeared to be an appropriate action. It saved some jobs in the United States, and also created new jobs in China and other foreign countries, where most all parts are being manufactured and even assembling of cars are now being performed in order to compete with $2/hr. foreign labor. There seems to be no chance of regulating big business to help the working class these days.

We Need A Redistribution of the Wealth

The Occupy Wall Street citizens know that there is something wrong when one percent of the people in this country own about seventy-five percent of the assets of the United States. Big business investor money that controls our government has been able to reduce the standard of living of the working class citizens to a new low with their latest innovation of replacing American workers with cheaper foreign workers. This is morally wrong, and it is also economically wrong. They are able to accomplish this because both the Congress and the White House chose to not oppose the big business investors who give them large campaign contributions and other favors.

These days campaign funding is the key to most elections and the financial status of office holders.

This working class degrading process can be stopped and " promoting the general welfare" can be restored if the working class citizens agree to not vote in any elections until complete campaign election reform is accomplished whereby all expenses are paid by taxpayer funds. Our current votes are not worth much because on economic issues most office holders actually represent the big business investors that fund them.

Our Trend Toward
Financial Occupations

In recent years there has been a big change in the types of occupations engaged in by the citizens of the United States. In past years people would seek jobs concerning production of a product or service that had a value that was evident, like farming, manufacturing and education. These days there is a huge movement toward occupations involving financial transactions. These jobs offer larger compensations and usually require less effort. They are even better if the activities are based upon pure money manipulation without having to provide something of value in the way of a product or service. One good example is that of a futures traders who merely bids on products like oil without ever taking delivery of the product. Another is that of an investment broker, who gambles with other people's money without any risk to the broker. These occupations permit people and companies to create money like they have a government printing press. All of this causes extreme inflation, which has been devastating to the working class citizens. As the big corporations replace American workers with cheaper foreign workers more jobs involving money manipulation are initiated. A true democracy would not permit these types of occupations. A plutocracy (money driven) would.

Keystone Pipeline Controversy

The Republican politicians are promoting the proposed Keystone pipeline. They claim that it will make more oil available and will help reduce the high price of gasoline. Politicians receive large contributions and favors from big business investors for such actions that permit the investors to exploit the working-class citizens. The purpose of a pipeline from Canada to the Gulf is to export that oil to other countries to receive the highest price available in the global market. Even if the oil was sold in the United States it would not resolve our problem because our high prices are primarily due to futures traders and oil company price gouging. Currently the supply of oil is high and the demand is low, which proves that the only solution is to eliminate the futures traders and the price gouging. The White House and the Congress will not interfere with the activity of the big business investors and lose their campaign contributions and other favors. To resolve this, and most of our economic problems, we must first obtain complete campaign finance reform where the taxpayers finance all elections.

Politicians Thrive by Deceiving the Public

The Republicans are proposing to ease the regulations concerning business investment occupations, ignoring the fact that they actually need more regulation to protect the public. These are some of the people that are making money but are not giving anything of value

in return. Republican's get about 80% of the
contributions from big business investors, so they
do more for them than the Democrats who only do
about 20% of the exploitation of the working
class. The cycle of profit-making by raising prices
is at the down-swing stage of the operation for oil,
gas and home prices. They needed to lower
prices so they can start the price-increasing phase
that gives them the greater profits. Futures
traders also participate in the same type of
operation to fleece the public. Politicians
also promote free enterprise to help big business
exploit the working- class citizens. The solution to
this devastating unregulated activity is to take the
money out of politics or, better yet, to eliminate the
occupation of politicians. .

The End

www.ingramcontent.com/pod-product-compliance
Lightning Source LLC
Chambersburg PA
CBHW060239290526
45789CB00001B/113